A Starting-Point Travel Guide

Zürich, Switzerland
And the Lake Zürich Region

Barry Sanders – writing as:

B G Preston

Zürich, Switzerland

Copyright © 2025 by B G Preston / Barry Sanders

All rights reserved. No part of this book may be reproduced or transmitted in any form or by any means without written permission from the author via his Facebook page or cincy3@gmail.com. The author's Facebook page may be found at: www.Facebook.com/BGPreston.author. Comments on this work and others are invited.

ISBN: 9798884331655

1st edition – Updated April 2025

Acknowledgements: The author greatly appreciates Sandra Sanders' contributions and guidance.

Photography: Maps and photos in the Starting-Point Guides are a mix of those taken by the author, Adobe Media, Shutterstock, Wikimedia, and Google maps. No photograph or map in this work should be used without checking with the author first. [1]

---

[1] This art, which is used throughout this guide, is the *Zurich Coat of Arms.*

Forward and Some Notes from the Author on the
Starting-Point Guides Approach and Coverage

What we look for in a travel guidebook can vary by each individual. Some travelers want great details into the history of every monument or museum, others may want details on area restaurants. This guide's coverage is a bit broader in approach. The goal of every Starting-Point Guide is to help orient you to the city and area and to gain an understanding of its layout, how to get around and highlights of the town's treasures, and what is nearby.

Overviews are provided on the town, suggested lodging, points-of-interest, travel, and the area. A moderate level of details is provided on restaurants and shops or museums and other points of interest.

The end goal is for you to come away from your visit having a good understanding of what is here, what the town is like, and not feel that you have missed out on leading sights and attractions.

Happy Travels, *B G Preston*

Chapters & Content

Preface 6

1: Zurich Introduction 15

2: When to Visit 28

3: Traveling to Zurich 33

4: City & Area Passes and Tours 40

5: Getting Around in Zurich 49

6: Where to Stay in Zurich 57

7: Points of Interest in Central Zurich 67

8: Points of Interest – Slightly Further Out 81

9: Lake Zurich, Ferries & Boat Tours 94

10: Easy Day Trips from Zurich 99

Appendix: Helpful Online References 122

Index 128

Starting-Point Travel Guides 130

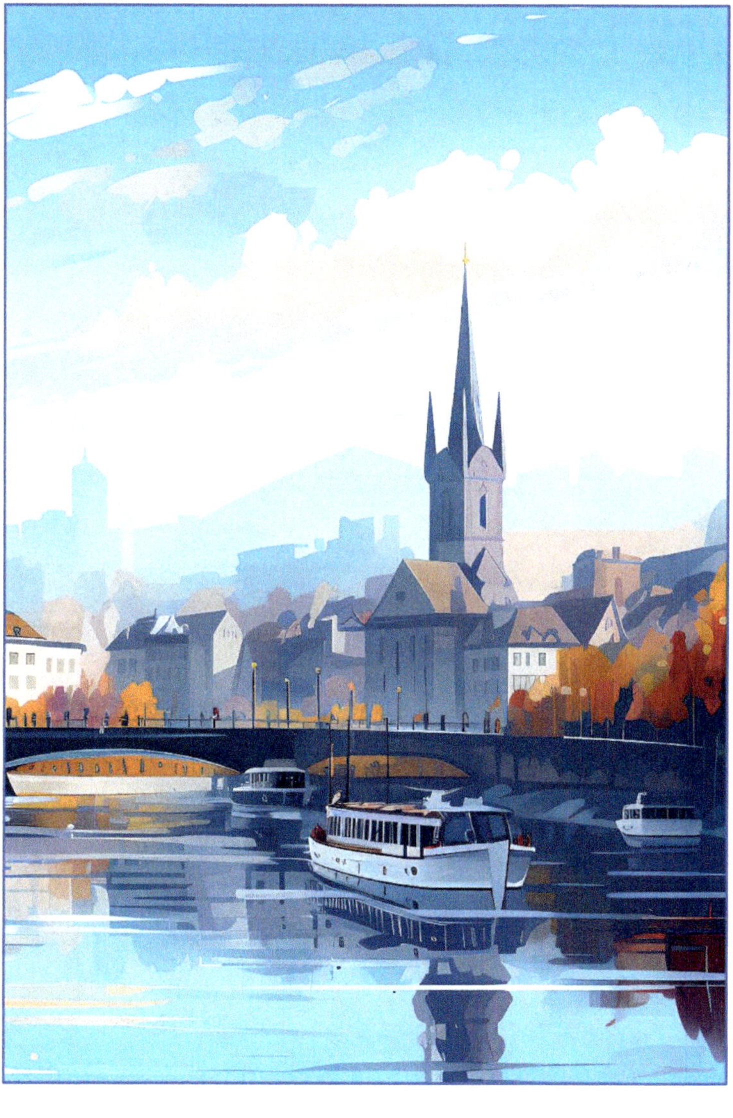

Preface
Area Covered & Some Suggestions

This Starting-Point Guide on Zurich is intended for travelers who wish to really get to know a city and area and not just make it one quick stop on a tour through Switzerland or Europe[2]. Oriented around the concept of using Zurich as a basecamp, this

Central Zurich is bisected by the Limmat River

---

[2] **One Day Itinerary**: While the focus of this guide is using Zurich as a basecamp for several days, the author realizes that many visitors will only be able to devote one day here. With this in mind, suggestions for a one-day visit are included in this chapter.

Preface

handbook provides guidance on sights both in the city and in the surrounding Lake Zurich region.

Area Covered in this Guide: While the focus and majority of coverage in this guide is on the city of Zurich and the neighboring area, several other enjoyable locales are presented as well. Opportunities range from mountain adventures, visits to a small country, and visits to nearby charming towns.

> A separate chapter is included on the sights along Lake Zurich – and the wonderful ferry system.

Each of these destinations may be reached easily from Zurich and, in many cases, by local train or tram services. In all cases, a trip to these attractive and varied destinations may easily be done in a relaxing day.

Area Covered in this Guide

- Rhine Falls
- Zurich
- St. Gallen
- Lake Zurich
- Liechtenstein
- Lucerne & Mt. Pilatus

Destinations Covered in this Guide
(In addition to Zürich)

Locale	Nature of Locale	Chp
Lake Zurich	This large lake is lined with small towns and even a world-famous chocolate factory. Plus, travel on the lake by ferry is just plain fun.	9
Local Mountains	Instead of spending the day traveling to world-famous mountains, check out the enjoyable mountain adventures right next to Zurich.	
Lichtenstein	Travel to Europe's 4th smallest country for a pleasant day's jaunt	
Lucerne	A picture-perfect town less than an hour south from Zurich with easy to reach mountain vistas.	10
Rhine Falls	Close to the border with Germany is a set of spectacular low falls on the Rhine River with a charming set of towns nearby.	
St. Gallen	A historic, colorful, nearly car free, Old Town with a Baroque cathedral. Easy to combine with a visit to Liechtenstein or Rhine Falls.	

Itinerary Suggestions: If your travel schedule allows, plan on staying at least 2 nights in Zurich. Ideally, you will be able to stay as many as three nights.

This is an area with a wonderful variety of points of interest such as the many sights right in town, nearby mountains, or lake explorations. Two or more days are needed to gain even a moderate understanding of what this area has to offer.

Strive to leave one day open and unplanned near the end of your stay. Build in a day in which you have not pre-booked any excursions or planned major activities. The reason for this is that, once there, you will discover places which you either want to revisit or learn about new places which appeal to you. If you have a full schedule, you will lose this luxury.

Head up to the Uetilberg for 360 views of Zurich.

One Day in Zurich: First and foremost, stay in or close to the center of town. If you only have one day here, spending that day traveling to such locations as Lucerne or to one of the mountain tops will give you little or no exposure to this beautiful and vibrant city. If you do want to spend your day getting out of the city, take a look at the chapters later in this guide which outline mountain adventures and some suggested day trips.

> **No Hop-On/Hop-Off Bus.**
> Unlike many cities, there is no Hop-On type of bus in Zurich. Given that most sights are in a small area, there simply is no need for this service.

Consider, for your one day here, following one of these three suggested approaches:

Old Town Zurich
A Great Place to Start Your Explorations.

- **City Highlights** – The "star" of Zurich is the Old Town area. Consider using this area as your focal point and explore from here. At the risk of sounding like a promotion for the Tourist Office, there is a lot here and there truly is something for everyone. Museums, beautiful shoreline, historic buildings, shopping, and more. But you may want to get out and see more than the tourist-centric heart of town and the next two approaches will help with this.

  > Enjoy Sports?
  > The FIFA World Football Museum is here.

  Consider a half-day tour. You probably won't want to spend all of your day bunched up with a group of others, being shown around the town by a guide, but doing this for a short two-to-four-hour tour can greatly enhance your understanding of Zurich. There are many, many options available and Chapter 4 helps with finding the best resource for you.

- **City and Lake** – Author favorite. There are many boat tours departing from Zurich's lakeshore. Take a look at Chapter 9 for some help with this. A wonderful way to experience the area, and not just the city, is to take one of the boat tours and many are short. This will give you an appreciation of the area beyond what simply strolling around the town on foot can do. Oh, and some of these tours include a stop at the Lindt Chocolate factory.

Lake Zurich Cruises - Many Options Are Available

- **City and Mountain** – You are in Switzerland and there is a natural tendency to want to spend your day up on a mountain. The downside to this is that for the "big name" destinations, it can easily take a full day to do this, taking away much of your opportunity to get to know Zurich. However, there are a few low mountains very close to central Zurich and it is easy to mix-and-match your mountain adventure with some town explorations for your one day here. Chapter 10 provides a list of several mountains which are close to Zurich. In addition to these mountains, you can also visit tall hills close to town. One of the best opportunities is to visit Ueitilberg. What you get from spending a few hours on this type of adventure are great views, few crowds, and the chance to take a short hike while still close to the city.

Consider a City, Region, or Country Travel Card: Zurich, like most cities, offers a travel card which provides discounts on local transportation, museum benefits, and more. IF, and only if, you will likely be visiting multiple attractions or using the transportation system for several trips, then consider purchasing one of the available cards.

Several options are available ranging from the *Zürich Card* to the *Swiss Travel Pass* along with other discount programs as well. These cards can be expensive, but they do offer convenience and, if actively used, some noteworthy savings.

Chapter 4 outlines the available cards

Visit the Tourist Office: Zurich's main Tourist Information Office is in the central train station on the ground floor. There is not, as of this writing, an office in central Zurich or the Old Town. So, if you arrive by train strive to take time to stop in here before you begin your adventures.

> Zurich Tourist Office Website:
> **www.Zuerich.com**

Obtain information on available tours and places to visit. Even if you have done substantial research prior to your trip, it is likely you will learn of opportunities which you had not previously uncovered. This is a good place to purchase the *Zürich Card* and even make tour arrangements.

Download Some Apps: With the incredible array of apps for Apple and Android devices, almost every detail you will need to have a great trip is available up to and including where to find public toilets. The following are a few apps used and recommended by the author.

Zurich Specific Apps:

- Zurich City Guide: If you download only one app for your visit here, this should be it. Provided by the tourist office with details on the Zurich Card, transportation, shopping, museums, and more.

- Zurich Transit – Excellent resource for the area's comprehensive transportation system. Provided by ZVV, Zurich's transportation company.

- Zurich Map and Walks: This firm, GPS My City, provides "map and walks" apps for numerous cities. They are great to help you find your way around town and locate shops, restaurants, and other points of interest.

Zürich City Guide App

Switzerland Travel and Helpful Information:

- SBB Trains: The Swiss national train system. Schedules, routes, and ability to purchase train tickets.

- Swiss Events: The app provides updated information on thousands of small and large events throughout the country.

- Switzerland Mobility: Details on hiking, biking, and cross-country skiing throughout Switzerland including trail details.

- Swiss Travel Guide: Similar to the SBB Trains app, but broader in that it includes bus, ferry, and train schedules along with details on key attractions.

- Swiss Travel Pass: The perfect app and service to use for travel by almost every mode of transportation in Switzerland. One caution, the pass is expensive.

General Travel Apps:[3]

- Rome2Rio: An excellent way to research all travel options including rental cars, trains, flying, ferries, and taxis. The app provides the ability to purchase tickets directly online.
- Trip Advisor: Probably the best overall app for finding details on most hotels, restaurants, excursions, and attractions.
- Flush: A very helpful app which provides guidance on where to find public toilets.

Currency Note: Switzerland is one of the few countries in Europe which uses its own currency, the *Swiss Franc.* As with most locations, the use of actual cash is fading. It can help to have a small supply of the local currency on you when you are in this country. For example, some restrooms require the use of local cash to use the facilities.

Consider just stepping over to an ATM at the airport or train station when you arrive at your first Swiss city.

The exchange rate is very close to an even rate with the Euro. As of this writing, for example, the rate is 1 Swiss Franc (CHF) = 1.05 Euro.

---

[3] **General Travel Apps:** There are numerous excellent travel apps to select from. The ones cited here are recommended by the author, but your search for helpful apps should not be limited to this.

1: Zurich[4] Introduction

Try a word association game with your friends and simply ask them to give their impression of Zurich in one word. Chances are you will hear responses like; finance, banking, rich, sophisticated, expensive, or classy.

The Old Town (Altstadt) District - is on both sides of the Limmat River.

---

[4] **Zurich or Zürich?** This city is within the German-speaking section of Switzerland. As a result, the formal German spelling is **Zürich.** However, given that Zurich is commonly used for English, the author will use this variation unless Zürich is the formal name of a location. Just as the word "Switzerland" is used instead of the German variation "Schweiz."

They would be right, but these terms are not the limit to what this largest city in Switzerland is. You could also add in any number of descriptors such as: mountainous, historic old town, modern city, beautiful lake, shoppers paradise, active, outdoorsy, and much more. The chapters in the guide will touch on many of these elements.

> **Not the capital of Switzerland.**
> Zurich is Switzerland's largest city – but it is not the capital. Bern is this country's capital.

Another term to describe Zurich is "central." You are a short drive or train trip from beautiful cities, mountain top adventures, other countries, outdoor adventures, and more.

Although Zurich has several impressive museums and historic sights, the real star of the show is the city's overall setting, the Old Town (Altstadt) and lake shore areas. If you do nothing more than just take time to wander around the heart of Old Town Zurich and perhaps have lunch at one of the restaurants overlooking the lake or river, you will come out a winner.

Zurich's Old Town/Altstadt is characterized by narrow avenues lined with restaurants and shops.

Zurich is a city of 415,000 people in the city. It is spread out over much of the lake and surrounding area and its overall urban population is a bit over 1.3 million. While it is near the heart of Switzerland, the setting is nowhere near as alpine as first-time visitors may expect. To be fair, this is an area with many low mountains, but the true Alps experience sits a bit further off in such towns as Lucerne or Interlaken.

> The low range of mountains adjacent to Zurich are the "Albis Mountains." The highest peak here is 2,858 feet.

Zurich Elevation. Given the mountainous image of "all things Switzerland", it can come as a surprise to learn that the elevation of this city is only 1,339 feet (408 meters). Much of the city and its neighborhoods (districts) sit on the hills which border the city center with the highest city elevation at 2,858 feet.

This is a non-hectic, but active city. Yes, there are some quaint, pedestrian-friendly areas, but the true essence of Zurich is commerce. The good news is that you never have the big city feel here as the overall character is inviting and tall business buildings are few.

Ride the Polybahn in central Zurich
Photo Source: Kevin B - Wikimedia Commons

What to Expect: Despite the photos depicting an attractive Old Town, this city is a vibrant mix of old and new. Other Swiss cities such as Lucerne, are geared toward tourism. In Zurich, while tourism is important, it is just one of several leading industries. So, what does that mean for your visit? It means that you will not confront as many tour bus groups as you might elsewhere, and you will likely feel more like you are visiting a "normal" city. That city, by the way, just happens to be nestled in a beautiful valley and is surrounded by inviting nature at every turn.

There are definite neighborhoods here each with their own character. Some, such as the Old Town, are more oriented to tourism, while other areas are more business-like or entertainment centric.

The Bahnhofstrasse - A Popular Shopping Street in Central Zurich
Photo Source: Sidonius - Wikimedia Commons

Zurich Introduction

Zurich Layout & its Districts: Many cities have distinct sections of town, each with their own characteristics and Zurich is no exception. When you visit here, you may soon hear references by name or a specific number such as "District 1" or "Zurich West."

> Several districts are typically referred to simply by their number.

In Zurich, there are twelve districts[5] which are laid out in something of a circular pattern, not unlike the arrondissements you would encounter in

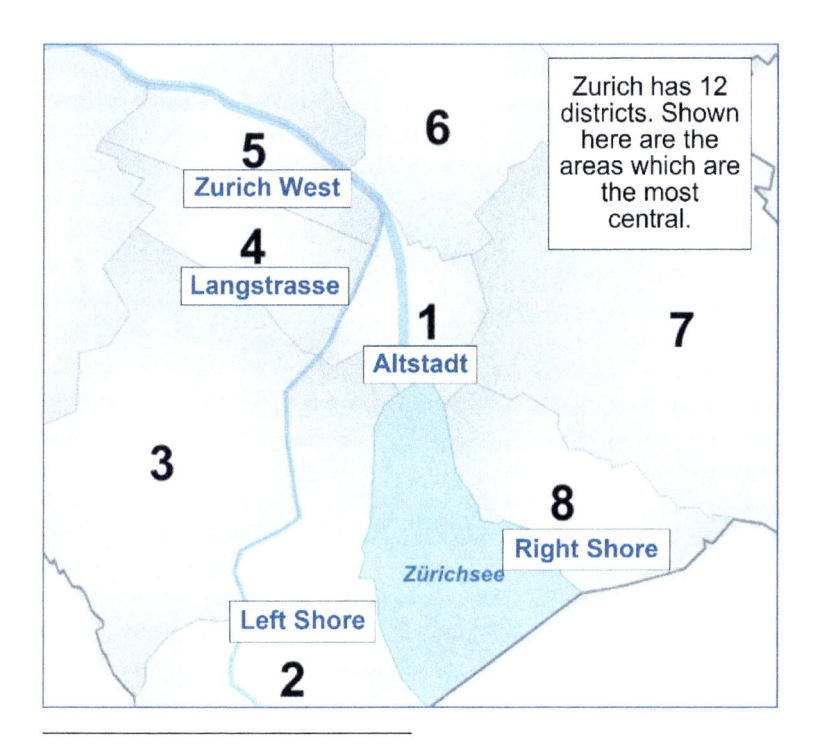

Zurich has 12 districts. Shown here are the areas which are the most central.

- 5 — Zurich West
- 6
- 4 — Langstrasse
- 1 — Altstadt
- 3
- 7
- 8 — Right Shore
- Zürichsee
- Left Shore
- 2

---

[5] **Districts, Quarters, & Neighborhoods:** In Zurich, these terms are not fully interchangeable. A "District" is the largest section of town. Within that, each District has "Quarters," and these can be as few as one or as many as 4 within a district. The term "Neighborhood" is often used instead of Quarter. For a bit of sanity and simplicity, this guide will limit geographical definitions to "Districts."

Paris. This puts District 1, Old Town in the heart of it all and other districts spiraling out from there.

Having a high-level understanding of the various sections of the city can be helpful for navigation and knowing what may be found in each part of the city.

District 1 – City Center / Altstadt: Also typically referred to as "Old Town" although only portions of District 1 truly fit this image. This is where you will likely spend much of your time while here. The Limmat River runs through the center. The main train station is here, along with the main shopping street of Bahhofstrasse, and major points of interest including St. Peter's Church.

District 2 – Western / Left Shore: Also referred to as either Enge or Wollishofen (two of the larger neighborhoods here). First, to avoid some confusion, you will likely see references to the Enge train station here in various maps or apps. This is an active station here, but it is not Zurich's primary train station. Come to this section of town for waterfront adventures, a wide array or restaurants and nightlife, and large park areas. One of the city's larger museums, the Museum Rietberg is here.

The long shoreline along Zurich Enge (District 2) provides many opportunities to enjoy the lake.
Photo Source: Roland ZH - Wikimedia Commons

District 3 – Wiedikon & Uetilberg: This is largely a residential area, but it sits at the base of the popular Uetilberg mountain adventure. By far, the most popular destination here is the trip up the mountain which is easily reached by local transportation. Chapter 8 provides more details on Uetilberg.

District 4 – Langstrasse: There is not a lot in the way of tourist attractions, museums, and such here. However, if you enjoy an active and diverse night life or an area which is deemed "trendy" with a variety of restaurants, head here. By the way, what remains of Zurich's red-light district is here as well. (This is legal in Switzerland.)

District 5 – Zurich West: Similar in some ways to District 4. This section of town was an industrial center. It has been undergoing a major transformation and, like District 4, you will find a good variety of shops and restaurants here. One of the popular destinations (bring money) is the restaurant Prime Tower near the top and with great views of the city below you. Another good

The Dolderbahn
A scenic uphill journey in Zurich's 6th District.
Photo Source: Patrick Nouhailler - Wikimedia Commons

destination is the large market hall, the "Markthalle Viadukt" which sits under the railway arches near the main train station.

Districts 6 & 7: Often referred to as Zurich's University area. Several universities are in this area including the large University of Zurich and ETH Zurich. ETH Zurich was Einstein's Alma Mater. This is an area with low rolling hills and a mix of residential and business plus the universities. Top attractions here include the zoo and a popular funicular, the *Dolderbahn Rack Railway*.

District 8 – Seefeld: Consider this the "high rent" section of town with some beautiful homes and many relaxing destinations such as the Opera House and the botanical garden. The greatest delight for many is the waterfront attractions including swimming spots and boat rentals.

Zurich's Eastern Lake Shore Area
District 8 - Seefeld
Photo Source: Roland ZH - Wikimedia Commons

Zurich Introduction

Zurich's Center: In all probability, much of your time here will be spent in, or close to central Zurich. This is where many of the better hotels are, popular shopping areas, attractive plazas, and some of the leading attractions. The area measures roughly 1 mile north-to-south and about ½ mile wide.

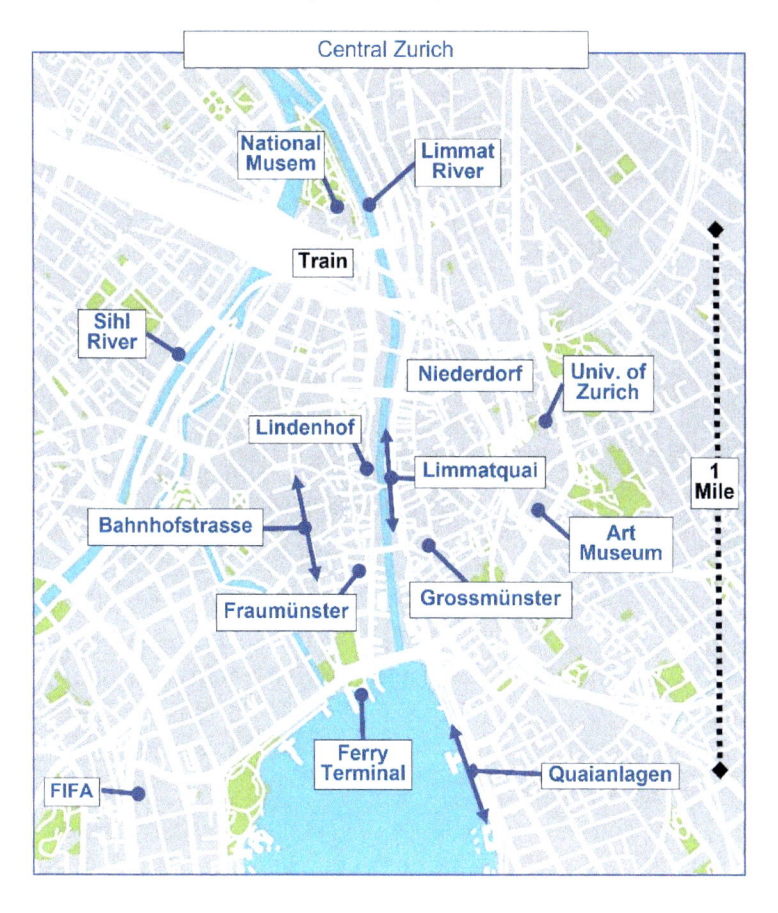

Central Zurich

- National Musem
- Limmat River
- Train
- Sihl River
- Niederdorf
- Univ. of Zurich
- Lindenhof
- Limmatquai
- 1 Mile
- Bahnhofstrasse
- Art Museum
- Fraumünster
- Grossmünster
- Ferry Terminal
- Quaianlagen
- FIFA

The biggest exceptions for central Zurich will be such events as a trip up the Uetilberg mountain overlook or to the zoo. In every case, reaching the points of interest in this city is easy to do via local transportation. Chapter 5 provides further guidance on getting around and Chapters 7 & 9 give greater detail on the leading attractions.

Some of Central Zurich's Highlights	
(See Chapters 7 & 8 for details)	
Name	What is Here
Bahnhofstrasse	Zurich's main shopping street.
Ferry Terminal	The primary location to catch ferries to other lake towns and boat tours. Also has a nice park.
FIFA Museum	FIFA Football/Soccer Museum
Fraumünster	Evangelical church with Marc Chagall windows.
Grossmünster	Protestant Church
Kunsthaus Zürich	Large art museum
Limmatquai	Long riverfront lane. Numerous restaurants with views of the river.
Lindenhof	Viewpoint in Old Town
Niederdorf	Medieval section of Old Town
Quaianlagen	Waterfront and park area. A great place to rent a small boat or go swimming.
Swiss National Museum	Swiss History & Culture Museum

Where to Start? Consider heading to the left bank (western side) of the river and up to the viewpoint at Lindenhof. This is a small park which sits on top of a former Roman fort. Today, it provides excellent views of central Zurich. A plus is to watch the river Limmat below you with the array of boat traffic. From here, it is easy to spot areas of interest and almost any point in central Zurich is a short walk.

View from Lindenhof Overlook in Central Zurich
Photo Source: Ank Kumar - Wikimedia Commons

Some Varied Facts and Background About Zurich:

- **Zurich Canton:** Switzerland is comprised of 26 cantons. Think of these as U.S. States or Canadian Provinces. Many of these had been independent areas until they were aligned under the Swiss Confederation with the most recent alignment occurring as recently as 1979.

    The city of Zurich is the capital of the Canton with the same name. This is the largest canton in population. Bern is the second largest. In geographical size, it is the second largest in Switzerland and Bern is the largest with almost three times the area.

- **City Name with Roman Roots:** When the Romans were here and established a small fort, they named the city *Turicum*. Through various twists and turns and pronunciation differences in various languages, this evolved into Zurich.

- **Roman Ruins:** In 1983, the remains of former Roman baths were discovered during a construction project. This is now open to public view in Old Town on the left bank, near St.

- **WWII Bombing:** Despite Switzerland's neutrality and non-intervention in major world wars, Zurich was the site on an accidental bombing raid in WWII. In 1945, six US B24s dropped bombs on the city. This had been the result of a navigational error as the flight crew thought they were over Germany. Unfortunately, this was not the only bombing raid on Switzerland in the war.

- **Water Fountains:** Throughout Zurich, you will encounter a variety of water fountains, roughly 1,200 of them. They vary in shape and history ranging from ancient to modern. The city prides itself on the cleanliness of its water, so feel free, have a drink of fresh Swiss water.

- **Quality of Life:** Zurich consistently ranks among the top cities in the world for overall quality of life. This evaluation includes such factors as healthcare, education, infrastructure, environment, and political stability.

- **Most Expensive:** So, now for the bad news, this city may have a top-notch quality of life, but there is a price to pay for it. In most lists of Europe's most expensive cities, Zurich ranks at the top. Factors driving this include rent, utilities, dining, and shopping.

- **Lake Zurich and the Cty of Zurich:** Zurich sits at the northwestern tip of Lake Zurich (officially named Zürichsee). This is the point where the short Limmat River begins. In size, the lake stretches for 25 miles (40 km). This lake remains narrow for its full length with the widest point being three miles wide. Its depth averages 161 feet (49 feet). See Chapter 9 of this guide for suggested Lake Zurich destinations.

- **Banks, Money, and Zurich:** We have all heard about Swiss Banks and the rumors are true. This city has been and continues to be a major financial powerhouse. It is, even today, considered to be a global hub for banking and wealth management. Major firms are located here such as Credit Suisse and UBS. As a result, this business sector is an important driver of employment with almost 6% of Swiss jobs being in financial services. (The only country with a higher percent of jobs in financial services is Singapore. Then the U.S. ranks third.)

- **Largest Church Clock:** Europe's largest church clock may be seen at the top of St. Peter's church. This church is in central Zurich on the left bank of the Limmat River.

- **Sports:** One fun aspect of traveling is to head off to a local game and experience sports in the city you are visiting. In Zurich, as with much of Europe, this means football (aka soccer). Zurich has a professional team FC Zurich. The current stadium, the Stadion Letzigrund, sits slightly west of the main train station. A new one is under construction as of this writing. For the game schedule, check their website: www.FCZ.ch

2: When to Visit
Climate & Major Events in and near Zurich

Climate in and near Zurich: A majority of the year here can have pleasant weather. Officially, the climate here is "moderately continental," which in casual terms means it can have cold winters and warm summers. There really isn't a bad season here. Yes, it can be cold in the winter, but it is also beautiful. With the excellent transportation in Switzerland, getting around town or out to nearby sights, is rarely problematic. The biggest variable which can add to some level of unpleasantness is crowds. However, tourist crowds in Zurich don't tend to be overwhelming.

Zurich in the Winter

Winter: This time of year, is often cold and grey. In fact, Lake Zurich does freeze over on occasion. The average annual snow fall in the city is about 33 inches (85cm). This may sound gloomy, but the city does take on a special charm during the winter, just bundle up some. A huge plus is that hotel rates tend to be low at this time of year. One factor, which is either a positive or negative depending on your perspective, is available tourist-related activities are few and many tours do not operate in the winter.

Spring: A perfect time to visit here. The climate is generally cool to mild although there can be some heavy rain brought in by the westerly winds. Crowds are moderate as are hotel rates. Keep in mind that "moderate" for Switzerland is still expensive. Tours and lake activities are opening up as are mountain trails for area day hikes. Another plus is the snowcapped mountains nearby provide some great photo opportunities.

Mountan Views from Lake Zurich

Summer: The climate in the summer tend to be pleasant with only moderate humidity. There are some rainy periods. Some can be heavy but, on average, this is the perfect time to go outdoors and just have fun. The one set of downsides, and they are noteworthy, is increased crowding and prices are at their max.

Fall: September to early October can bring near perfect conditions although rain showers are still common. Expect cool to warm temperatures. Most tours will still be in operation and the crowds will be moderate. Probably the ideal time to visit here.

Zurich Average Area Climate by Month [6]			
Month	Avg High	Avg Low	Avg Precip
Jan	38 F / 4 C	30 F /-1 C	2.5 inches
Feb	41 F / 5 C	30 F /-1 C	2.4 inches
Mar	50 F / 10 C	35 F /2 C	2.8 inches
Apr	59 F /15 C	41 F /5 C	3.1 inches
May	66 F /19 C	48 F /9 C	5 inches
Jun	72 F /22 C	55 F /13 C	5 inches
Jul	76 F /24 C	58 F /14 C	5 inches
Aug	75 F /24 C	58 F /14 C	4.7 inches
Sep	66 F /19 C	51 F /11 C	3.4 inches
Oct	57 F /14 C	45 F /7 C	3.3 inches
Nov	46 F /8 C	37 F / 3 C	3 inches
Dec	39 F / 4 C	31 F /-1 C	3.3 inches

Major Festivals and Events in & near Zurich: There are several popular events in this area each year. Visiting one of these can be a great addition to your stay. The only downsides are the added crowds in Zurich and increased lodging rates. Information

---

[6] **Weather Resource:** All climate data cited here is from Wikipedia.com

When to Visit

on some of the leading events follows. (This is not a complete list of all events.).[7]

When	Event
February or March	Züri-Carneval
April	Zurich Spring Festival
Mid-August	Street Parade (huge)
Early October	Zurich Film Festival
Late Nov thru Dec	Christmas Markets

Züri-Carneval: For three days in the winter (typically in late February or early March), the folks in Zurich let their hair down with a series of lively events. This is their version of Mardi Gras, and you can find numerous bands and music ranging from local to Latin American. www.ZurichCarneval.ch.

Zurich Spring Festival: One very lively day, typically in mid-April, with the intent of saying goodbye to winter. This is done with a huge parade followed by a large bonfire where winter is burned in Effigy. The event occurs in central Zurich. The official name is Sächsilüüte. (Pronounce this correctly and someone owes you a beer.)

The Tour de Suisse

If you are lucky, the Tour de Suisse could be occurring when you are in Switzerland. It can be a lot of fun to head out to the Swiss countryside to watch the bike race in action.
For details, the route and schedule check

www.TourdeSuisse.com

---

[7] Events in and near Zurich: The area's tourist website www.Zuerich.com provides updated details on most events here.

Street Parade: Dubbed as "The world's Largest Techno Party.". Put another way, come with a young spirit, open mind, and ear plugs. This massive event occurs for just one day in mid-August with lively music occurring through central Zurich. There is even a boat parade in addition to the 2 km long parade route. 2025 will be the 32nd running of this event. www.StreetParade.com

The Zurich Street Parade with Huge Crowds
Photo Source: Ricardo Hurtubia - Wikimedia Commons

Zurich Film Festival / ZFF: In early October, hundreds of films are shown during an 11-day period across Zurich. While this is held in several venues, the focal point is the Sechseläutenplatz plaza on the right (eastern) shore of the lake. This festival is simply referred to as the ZFF. For details and tickets check www.zff.com.

The Zurich Christmas Markets: As with almost every city in Europe, there are popular and inviting Christmas markets here. There are several locations to head to with the focal point being the Old Town. The main station is another great, and unexpected, locale as you can find one of Europe's largest indoor Christmas markets here.

~ ~ ~ ~ ~

3: Traveling to Zurich

Located in north central Switzerland, Zurich may seem somewhat isolated, but it really is not all that far from a good variety of cities small and large. Zurich is easy to reach by driving, train, or air from these cities and typically in just a few hours' time. [8]

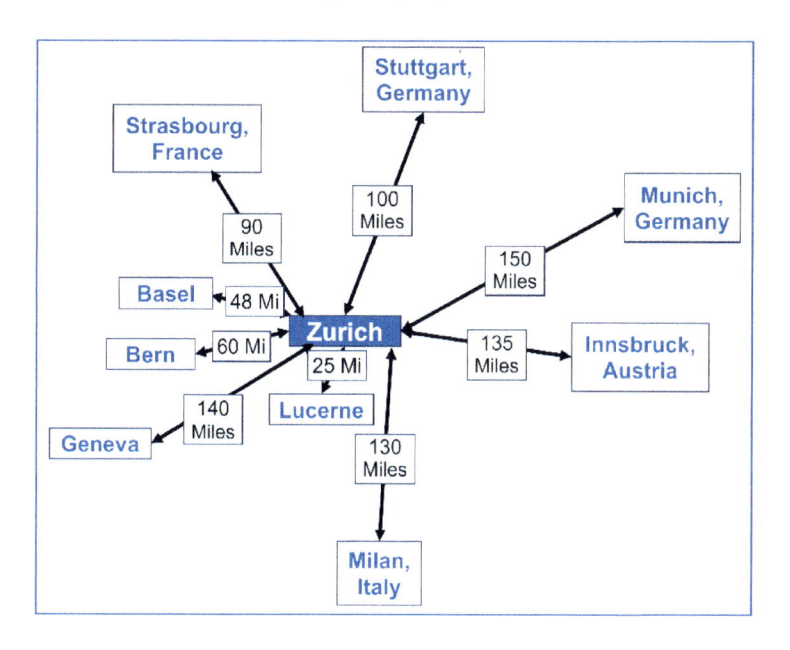

```
                    Stuttgart,
                    Germany
                       ↑
   Strasbourg,         |
   France              |              Munich,
      ↖           100 Miles           Germany
       90 Miles                          ↗
                                 150 Miles
      Basel ←─48 Mi─┐
                    Zurich ──135 Miles──→ Innsbruck,
      Bern ←─60 Mi──┘                     Austria
                    25 Mi
              140    ↓
   Geneva ←  Miles  Lucerne
                       |
                   130 Miles
                       ↓
                    Milan,
                    Italy
```

---

[8] **Distances Shown:** The distances cited on the above diagram are "as the crow flies" and will naturally vary based on your mode of transportation and your start and end points.

A Starting-Point Guide

Travel Planning App: When planning your travel, consider using one of the sites or apps which allow you to easily compare differing modes of transportation. One of the better services (not the only one) is www.rome2Rio.com. If you choose, you can also book travel directly from this site.

<blockquote>
Airport to Train Station Connector

To make transportation from the airport into Zurich easy, there is a dedicated train between the airport and train station which departs every 10 minutes.
</blockquote>

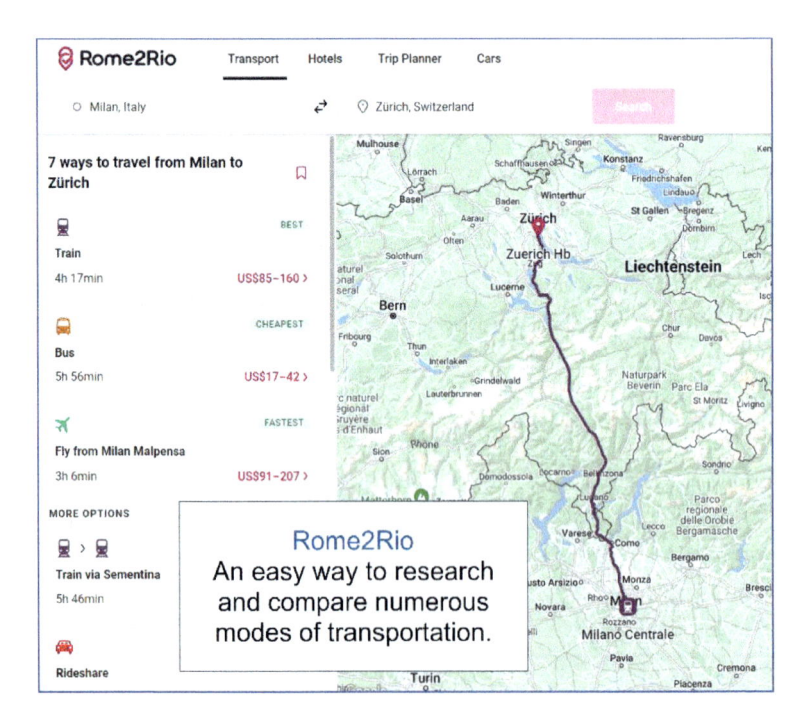

Rome2Rio
An easy way to research and compare numerous modes of transportation.

Arriving by Train: There is one major train station in central Zurich. Other stations are in the metro area but, in all likelihood, if you travel to or from here by train it will be to *Zürich HB*. The formal name of this station is Zürich Hauptbahnhof.

Zurich's Central Train Station
Adjacent to the Limmat River

The station is about as central to the heart of Zurich as you could want. The terminal abuts the river and is at the northern end of Zurich's Altstadt - Old Town. If you have booked lodging in central Zurich, there is a good chance that you could walk from the station to there. If you need local transportation, the city's trams and buses stop here.

One caution, this station is big, and it is busy. The track lines and various services are spread over multiple levels. Some of the services you can find here include a large shopping mall, Shopville, and the Tourist Office. There are also numerous restaurants here.

If you need storage lockers, these are also available.

For full details and layout of this station, check: www.SBB.ch – then navigate to the page on Zurich.

Some Acronyms:

You will see these identifiers frequently on trains and train services:

SBB – The main federal railway – the Swiss Bundesbahen.

FFS – The national railway company, the Ferrovie Federali

A Starting-Point Guide

Zurich's Central Train Station Location

Train Station

Limmat River

--- Altstadt / Old Town ---

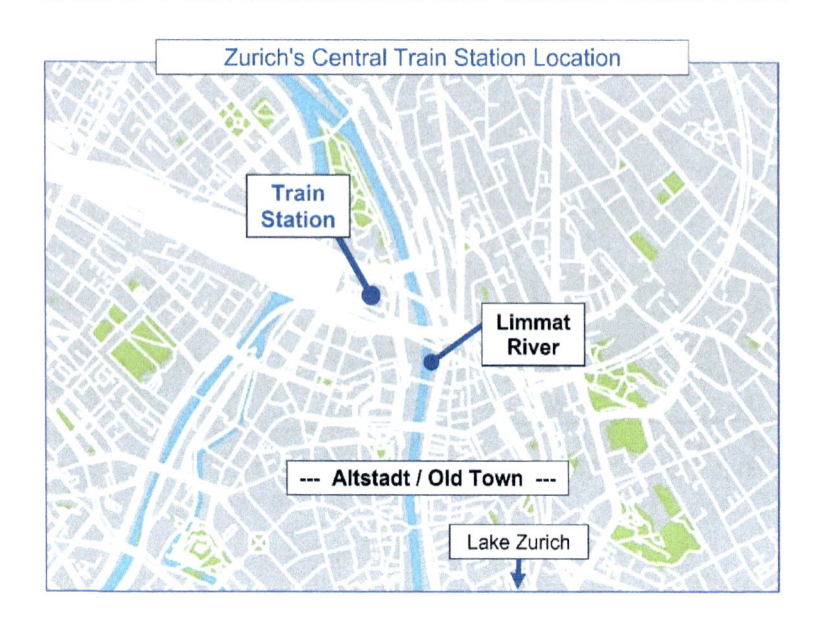

Lake Zurich

Typical Train Travel Time to Zurich from Nearby Cities		
City	**Travel Time[9]**	**Daily Trains**
Bern	1 hour	10+ per day
Geneva	2 hrs & 45 min	10+ per day
Innsbruck, Austria	3 ½ hours	5 to 10 per day
Lucerne	45 min	10+ per day
Milan, Itay	4 hrs & 20 min	5+ per day
Munich, Germany	3 ½ hours	5 to 10 per day
Strasbourg, France	2 hrs & 45 min	5 to 10 per day
Stuttgart, Germany	3 hours	5 to 10 per day

[9] **Train Travel Time:** This can vary dramatically depending on the train and route you select. The time shown here is something of an average for direct train routes.

Booking Train Tickets. Given the popularity of travel to Zurich, advance purchase should be considered, especially in high season. If you have not purchased train tickets in advance, convenient ticket booths are available at most train stations.

Several online services are available to book in advance including:

SBB.ch – Switzerland's national rail service. Using them provides the advantage of being able to make changes in the station if problems arise. This is also a good site to explore and purchase travel passes.

Ticket Resellers – Several online agencies allow you to book tickets through them and may provide the convenience of booking other forms of transportation or lodging at the same time. Leading resources for this include (And not limited to):

- www.rome2Rio.com (Author favorite)
- www.TrainLine.com
- www.RailEurope.com

~ ~ ~ ~ ~ ~

Arriving by Air: The Zurich airport, *Flughafen Zürich* is located roughly six miles north of the city. This is a big and busy airport and is Switzerland's largest. The airport is also the home base for Swiss International Airlines (Swiss Air). This airport is something of a hub for international transportation into the region and, as a result, it is well connected with ground transportation. It also has a fairly large shopping center right in the airport.

A Starting-Point Guide

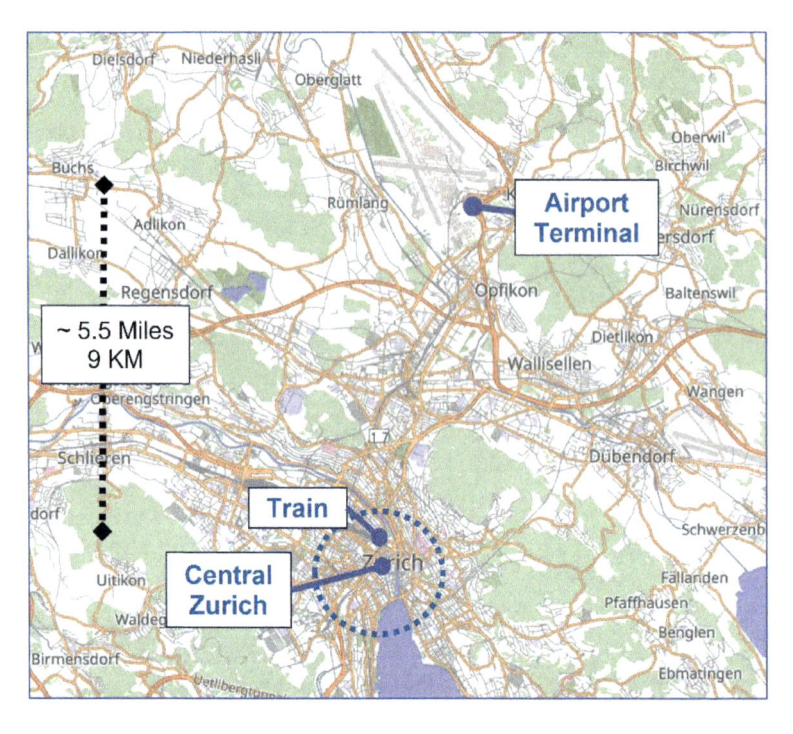

~ 5.5 Miles
9 KM

Airport Terminal

Train

Central Zurich

The **Switzerland info** offices in the airport can provide guidance on tours, passes, and more.
Photo Source: flughafen-zuerich.ch

Transportation from the Airport: In addition to the usual array of transportation into town from the airport, there is also a substantial train station which sits just below the ticketing and baggage areas. Not only can you get trains into central Zurich, but you can also catch trains to a large number of neighboring cities. This means that, if you are traveling to such places as Lucerne or Bern, you will likely be able to catch a train directly from the airport and not have to make a change in Zurich's main station.

Some notes on differing transportation options:

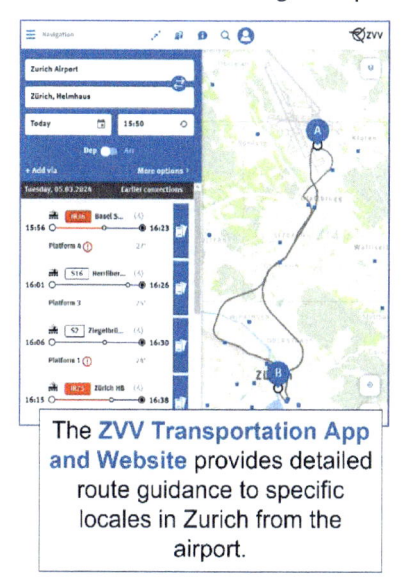

The **ZVV Transportation App and Website** provides detailed route guidance to specific locales in Zurich from the airport.

Train into Town[10] – A 10-to-15-minute ride to Zurich's central station. This train runs roughly every 10 minutes. Catch this train below the airport. Reservations are not needed.

Trams into Town – This can be slower than the trains as the journey will take around 30 minutes. This mode, however, can offer the advantage of taking you closer to your lodging or other destination. Use the ZVV Transportation app to determine the best route.

Taxi: In addition to the array of services such as UBER, a great area transportation service to consider is 7X7. (www.7x7.ch). You may reserve a car, limo, or van in advance with this service and they will be waiting for you at the arrivals area when you arrive.

---

[10] **Free with Zürich Card:** If you purchase this discount card in advance or from the Tourist Office in the airport, you may use the train or tram service into town for no additional cost.

4: City & Area Passes[11] and Tours

If you will be staying in Zurich for several days and wish to visit multiple attractions, then acquiring the *Zürich Card* can be a good idea. Another option, which focuses on transportation, is the *Swiss Travel Pass*. This country-wide pass is described further in this chapter. **Do not buy both.**

Zurich, like most cities in Europe, offers city passes that provide discounted or free admission to local transportation and many attractions. In Zurich, the pass includes access to area attractions, and discounts on tours, boat travel, and numerous local shops and restaurants.

Full details on this pass and what it covers may be found at www.Zuerich.com.

---

[11] **Passes Covered and Not Covered:** This guide focuses on the Zürich Card and the Swiss Travel Pass. Other passes are available but, are not outlined here as they are not as specific to Zurich or area travel. If you are interested in researching other pass options, consider looking into the Swiss Museum Pass and the Tell Pass.

City & Area Passes & Tours

Benefit Type	**Zürich Card**	**Swiss Travel Pass**
Card Comparison — General Benefits of the Zürich Card vs the Swiss Travel Pass			
Transportation in Zurich Metro	√	√
Transportation outside of Zurich	X	√
Museums in Zurich — Free or Discounted Admissions	√	√
Tours in Zurich — Discounts on local Tours	√	X
Restaurant & Shopping Discounts	√	X
Mountain Adventures — Discounts on notable mountain trips.	Limited	Many
Typical Cost for 3-day Pass[12]	CHF 56	CHF 244

Zürich Card Overview:

General Coverage and Who Should Use: The natural focus of this card is on attractions and transportation in and close to Zurich. Given this, consider acquiring this card only if: (a) you will be spending several days here; (b) will likely visit several attractions; and (c) you have not already purchased a country-wide Swiss Travel Pass.

If you are considering purchasing this pass primarily for the travel benefits, keep in mind that you can purchase an inexpensive 24-hour transportation pass from ZVV the local transportation agency. This can be done at almost any tram stop or online from Z-Pass.ch

---

[12] **Daily Cost Comparison:** Use this as a general guideline only. There are several price tiers for both pass types. This comparison is using rates as of early 2025 and for the 72-hour pass rate for one adult.

A Starting-Point Guide

Limmat River Cruises are Included in the Zürich Card
Photo Source: Zuerich.com

Duration & Age Variations: This card is available for either 24 hours or 72 hours. There is no 48-hour option as of this writing. Also, there are two rate tiers, adult and child.

Likely Rates: (As of April 2025 and subject to change):

Zürich Card Duration	Adult Rate	Child Rate
24 Hours	CHF 29	CHF 19
72 Hours	CHF 56	CHF 37

What is Included: These passes offer a mixture of free and discounted components such as:

- Local Transportation: Free unlimited use of the local public transportation services. This also includes bicycle rental.
- Museums: Free and reduced admission to most area museums.
- Tours: Discounts on several city tours such as an Old Town Walking Tour or a boat tour along the Limmat River.

City & Area Passes & Tours

- Restaurants: Discounts at several area restaurants.
- Shopping: Discounts in many area stores.
- Nearby Attractions: Free or reduced admission to such attractions as the local zoo, water park, and wilderness park.

Public Transportation: The pass is for unlimited 2nd-class travel on area transportation. This does not cover transportation to other cities such as Lucerne. Several local lake cruises and cable car trips up to Uetilberg are included within the transportation component of the card's benefits.

Timing: These passes are valid from when they are first used, not for a specific day. Even when you purchase a pass online, you are asked to state the hour and day you will first use the pass. So, for instance, if your first use is at 1PM on a Monday and you have purchased a three-day pass, that pass will be valid until 1PM on Thursday, three days later.

App: If you purchase this pass, downloading the app is advised as it provides a QR code to use for your first use, and includes details on every destination and service which accepts these cards. Also, the app is needed to take advantage of several services such as bicycle rental.

Where to Buy: The cards are available online via www.Zuerich.com, from the tourist office and also from several resellers such as MySwitzerland.com. Also, check with your hotel as several hotels in the area sell these passes as well.

Swiss Travel Pass (Previously called the "Swiss Pass") [13]

This popular travel pass allows you to use most of Switzerland's transportation system including trains, bus, and ferry systems, and many mountain lifts and gondolas.

> Children travel free when they are with an adult who has a Swiss Travel Pass.

When using this pass, separate reservations are not needed for train tickets, so this adds potential savings in travel cost and planning.

This pass also includes many museums, eliminating the need to purchase the Zurich Card for this benefit. With the Swiss Travel Pass, you may take an unlimited number of trips on included modes of transportation.

What it Covers:

- All of Switzerland
- Unlimited train travel
- Unlimited ferry travel
- Unlimited bus travel
- Free or discounted travel on select mountain rail and gondolas.
- 500+ museums, free entry.

Variations: A complex array of pass options are available.

- Class: Purchase passes for 1st or 2nd class travel.
- Days Covered: purchase passes for 3, 4, 6, 8, or 15 days.
- Flex or Standard days: Ticket options cover number of days as a group or flex.
  - Non-Flex: The number of days covered are in sequence.

---

[13] **Swiss Travel Pass vs the Swiss Pass:** The "Swiss Pass" is intended to be used only by Swiss residents. Visitors should consider the "Swiss Travel Pass."

- o Flex: The days purchased, such as 4 days, must be used within 1 month of purchase, but do not need to be used in sequence. This variation is more expensive.
- **Age of Traveler:** Two price tiers are available: Adults and "Youth" for individuals between 16-24 years old. The youth ticket's cost is roughly 70% of the adult rate.

Expensive
Caution – these passes are expensive, so do not purchase unless you will be able to use it on several trips.

Cost: Given the many variables, it is best to check the Travel Pass website to determine the cost of a pass which best fits your needs. Some price examples follow.

Swiss Travel Pass Price Examples
Adult Rates in Swiss Francs[14] as of early 2025 – subject to change

Days Covered	Standard		Flex Days	
	2nd Class	1st Class	2nd Class	1st Class
3 Days	CHF 244	CHF 389	CHF 279	CHF 445
4 Days	CHF 295	CHF 460	CHF 339	CHF 539
6 Days	CHF 379	CHF 602	CHF 405	CHF 644

How to Obtain: Order online. Several firms do sell these passes, but it is advised to purchase through the Swiss Pass site. When purchasing through www.Swiss-Pass.ch, it is much easier to resolve pass issues while in Switzerland than having to work

---

[14] **Swiss Franc:** The CHF (Swiss Franc) is typically close to, but not the same as, the Euro or USD in spending value.

through an online reseller. Purchase through www.Swiss-Pass.ch.

Zurich Tour Companies: If your schedule allows, consider taking one of the many tours within Zurich. These tours range from short 1- or 2-hour events to full-day explorations. Even if you are disinclined to join structured group events, at least one tour should be considered as they almost always enhance your understanding of the city, its history, and main attractions.

Several tours of interest will be available from the Tourist Office, and many may be purchased in advance.

Numerous online services enable you to explore available tours and purchase passes. These offerings often go well beyond those offered by the Tourist Office and some tours may be customized to your specifications.

Some of the leading tour providers are:[15]

- www.Zuerich.com – Zurich Tourist Office – go to the "Discover" section for a list of tours.

- www.WowZurich.com – A local tour firm offering a good variety of half- and full-day tours such as Lindt Chocolate Factory visits or combination boat and walking tours. Most are small groups with some private tours available.

- TripAdvisor.com – Search for Zurich and go to the "Things to do" page

- Viator.com (A service of Trip Advisor). Expansive list of tours in Zurich and to nearby areas. The list of tours cited here is similar to those found under Trip Advisor.

- GetYourGuide.com – Search for Zurich to view the provided tours which range from local walking tours to food tours and mountain excursions.

---

[15] **Tour Providers Note:** The providers cited here are a representative listing only. This is not intended to be a comprehensive list of firms which provide tour services in the area.

- ToursByLocals.com - This firm offers many private and small-group tours with a focus on private tours. They can be a bit expensive.

Example Zurich City Tours: Following is a list of several recommended tours. Most of these may be purchased from the Zurich Tourist Office. Many other tours are available through other companies such as those cited above. The Tourist Office is a great place to start your search for tours as they offer a full variety ranging from walking, historic, gastronomic, historical, and even whimsical tour offerings.

- City Tour Bus – (Not a hop-on bus) – 2 & ½ hour tour of the highlights in and close to central Zurich. Multiple photo opportunity stops along the way. Available from www.Zuerich.com.

- Old Town Walking Tour – Available from several providers including the Tourist Office. Also available as a private or group tour. Gain a detailed understanding of some of the city's history and prominent structures. The tours last about 2 hours.

- Tuk Tuk Old Town Tour – An interesting and relaxing way to ride through areas of Old Town which bus tours are not able to visit. Typically, a 90-minute tour and available from the Tourist Office or www.Etuktuk.ch.

> **Tours Out of Town**
> The tours outlined here focus on central Zurich. Many other tours take you to nearby mountains, the Rhine Falls, and even the small country of Lichtenstein. Most of these tours are full day. See Chapter 10 for some details on suggested day trips outside of Zurich.

- Lake Cruise & Lindt Chocolate Factory – An author favorite. Combine an enjoyable boat tour to gain great views of the city and then a guided tour through Zurich's most prominent chocolate factory. Portions of the travel are by bus. This is a 4- to 6-hour tour. Offered by Viator.com and others.

- Highlights of Zurich – Take a half-day private tour of central Zurich with a delightful mixture of cable cars, local ferry, and walking. Available from Viator.com.

- Uetilberg Mountain Excursion – Visit Zurich's tallest vantage point with a guide. The tour includes a short hike along with a small meal while you enjoy the views. Check Tours by Locals for details. Also, if you are interested in visiting this close mountain, check Chapter 8 for more information.

The above list is only a small sample of available tours which will help you become acquainted with Zurich. If you are seeking enjoyable day trip destinations, such as a trip to Lucerne, Mt. Rigi, Lichtenstein, and others, Chapter 10 provides more detail on these opportunities.

5: Getting Around in Zurich
Walking, Trams, Ferries, & Bicycles

When visiting Zurich, a majority of the historic sights are in one fairly small area, so transportation issues are not likely to be an issue. If, however, you will be here for more than one or two days, learning how to navigate the city's transportation options can be beneficial. Consider downloading one of the many apps, such as the Map and Walks App by GPS my City. Apps such as these provide suggested walks based on your interests and details on most attractions and even restaurants will be included.

Central Zurich is very easy to explore on foot or by tram.

Walking in Central Zurich: With the central area of town being only about 1 mile from north to south, most walking distances are fairly short. If you were to use the Limmat River in Old Town as your focal point, almost every destination is less than a 15-minute walk. Most of this is on fairly level ground and much of this can be on pedestrian-friendly stretches.

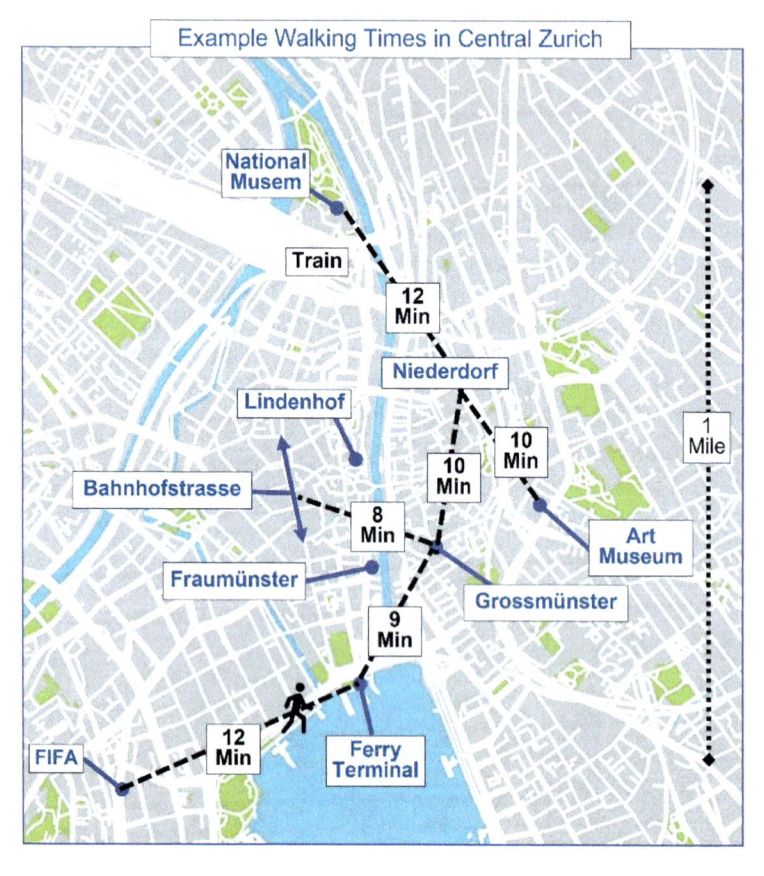

Example Walking Times in Central Zurich

Having the Limmat River right in the heart of central Zurich also adds the pleasant aspect of being able to do much of your strolling alongside the river (on the Limmatquai) or over one of the many bridges.

Getting Around in Zurich

The Zurich Map and Walks App is a good resource to help you navigate the city on foot.

Strongly advised – Download one of the apps such as the *Zurich Map and Walks app* to help guide you. Many of the streets in Old Town are narrow and can be a bit of a maze. Having an app which shows you exactly where you are and what is near you can be helpful and informative.

Trams, Buses, & Local Trains: There is an excellent array of ground-level trams[16], bus lines, ferries, and even a funicular to help you get around in Zurich. The array of transportation names and identities can be confusing at first and the fact that there is substantial overlap adds to the confusion. Basically, there are two major levels of transportation, each with their own identity. [17]

- **ZVV** – The ZVV transportation system is an all-encompassing transportation network for the canton of Zurich. (Cantons are similar to states within the U.S or provinces in Canada.) This network includes the regional train service, the S-Bahn trains. www.ZVV.ch

- **SBB** – This is the country-wide rail service. The focus of the SBB is trains, vs the ZVV which has a variety of local trains, buses, and trams.

SBB CFF FFS

---

[16] **Trams and Streetcars:** In Zurich, the trams are often referred to as Street Cars.

[17] **ZVV and VBZ** – To add to the confusion, a third level exists, the VBZ. This is a tram system which is owned by the city of Zurich and only covers the city. It operates within the ZVV network and accepts their tickets and passes, so you do not need to purchase separate passes before boarding a VBZ labeled tram.

A Starting-Point Guide

Use the SBB to travel to other cities in Switzerland. Also, SBB passes cover travel on the ZVV. (There are also other regional and nation-wide rail services operating in Switzerland. SBB passes typically are accepted on these lines.) www.SBB.ch

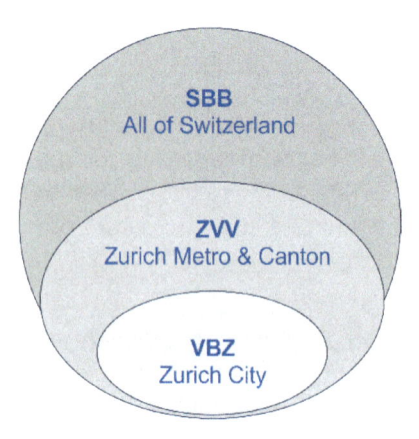

SBB — All of Switzerland

ZVV — Zurich Metro & Canton

VBZ — Zurich City

A Busy Tram Station in Central Zurich
Photo Source: Andreas Praefcke - Wikipedia

Understanding the System: Good news and bad news. On the "good news" front, this is an extensive system, and you can travel to almost any locale within the city on the local trams. The bad news is, given the complexity of the system with its fifteen, sometimes overlapping, lines, it can be difficult to learn. Also, not every line services the center of town.

Getting Around in Zurich

> The **ZVV App** is an essential tool for traveling in Zurich.

While route maps are shown at most tram stops, having an app handy is probably your best way to ensure you are hopping aboard the correct tram.

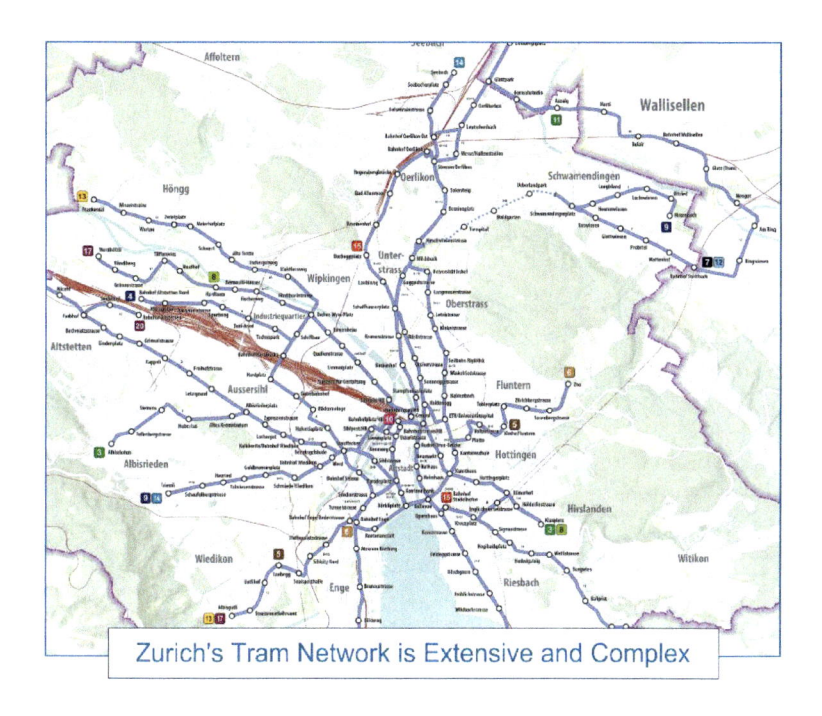

Zurich's Tram Network is Extensive and Complex

Tickets & Passes: Several ticket and pass options are available, and all may be purchased from one of the ticket machines at every tram stop. The bad news is that there are many, many variations available. So, while the ticket options may cover every possible contingency known to man, it can be overly complex. Oh, just to let you know, both the ZVV and Tourist Office websites claim that this is a simple and easy to learn the system… uh, no.

A Starting-Point Guide

Each ticket or pass type essentially has four variables:

- Geography / Zones: Zurich's transportation network is laid out by zones and many ticket options are based on the number of zones it covers. The good news is that most of the travel within central Zurich is all in the same zone, number 110. When purchasing a ticket, you will need to select if your travel will be in 1-2 zones up to all zones. By the way, some zones, such as Zurich's central 110 zone, count as two zones.

> Trams and Buses are Free if you have either the Zürich Card or Swiss Pass.
>
> If you have either of these passes, you may ride as many zones and for as many trips as you want with no further cost or decisions to make.

- Class of Tickets: You have the option of purchasing a 1st or 2nd class ticket.
- Age: Each ticket type has the choice of adult or child rates. (And, they are very exacting... a child rate covers ages up to 15.99 years... really.)
- Ticket Duration: Once you have determined where you want to travel, if you want to travel 1st or 2nd class, and if your child is under 15.99 years old, then the last decision is on the length of time you wish to travel. The two basic options are for a 1-hour ticket or a 24-hour ticket.

Where to Buy: This part really is simple. First, if you have a Zürich Card, all you need to do is have the pass stamped at the ticket machine for your first trip (or use the QR code if you have the app). Without a pass, you may either purchase tickets from ZVV.ch for Zurich area travel or from SBB.ch for travel in Zurich and the rest of the country. Also, and probably the easiest, you may simply buy your ticket from the machines found at almost every tram and bus stop.

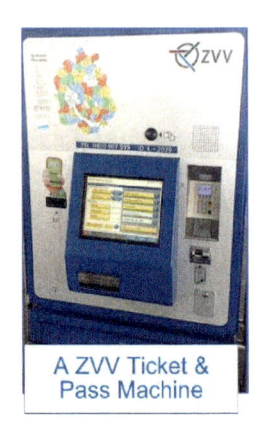

A ZVV Ticket & Pass Machine

Ferry Travel: While this mode of travel isn't really used within metro Zurich, it is a fun way to visit nearby lakefront communities. (See Chapter 9 for more info on Lake Zurich.) Most ferries depart from the dock at the southern section of the Old Town. These are mostly people ferries with only a few routes carrying cars. Also, most ferry travel is covered by the Zürich Card or the Swiss Travel Pass.

The service is under the identifier of ZSG and full details of available ferry routes may be found at www.Zsg.ch.

A Lake Zurich Ferry
Photo Source: Roland zh - Wikipedia

Bicycle Rental: Much of Zurich can easily be explored on bicycle. With the areas near the lake and Old Town on flat land, it is easy to find an enjoyable and relaxing route.

There are several firms which provide bicycle and e-bike rentals. By far, the largest service is Züri Velo, which is operated by PubliBike. This service from PubliBike is available under different brand names in several towns across Switzerland. This is helpful as you only need to set up one account with PubliBike and use one app to be able to use this bicycle rental service across the

A Starting-Point Guide

country even with the service being under different local brand names such as Züri Velo.

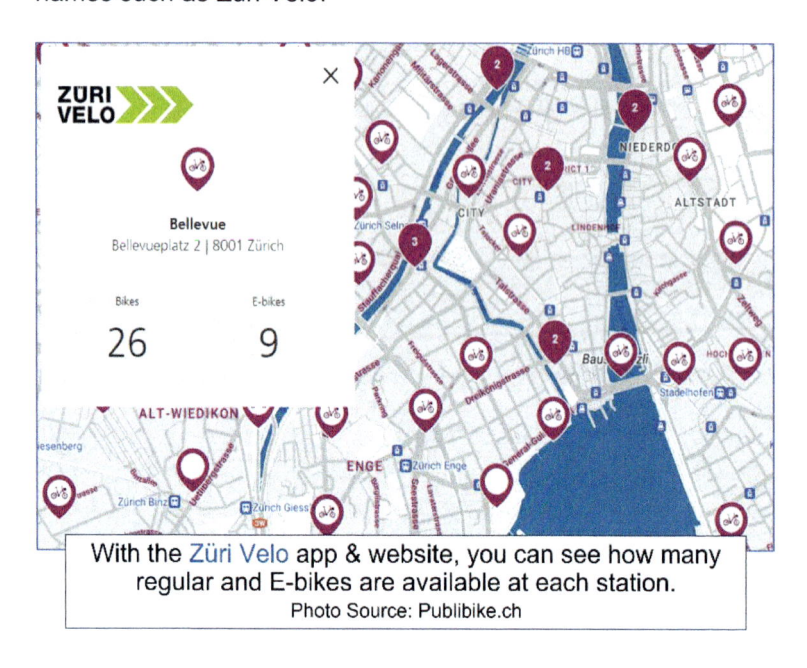

With the Züri Velo app & website, you can see how many regular and E-bikes are available at each station.
Photo Source: Publibike.ch

In Zurich, there are dozens of Züri Velo rental stations throughout the metropolitan area. To rent a bicycle from this service, you will need to use the app or website to set up an account then use the app to rent the bicycle. Bikes may be returned to any station with available docking slots. The app will indicate if bikes are available to rent and, when you are ready to return, which stations have open slots to return your bike.

Website: www.PubliBike.ch

6: Where to Stay in Zurich

Quality lodging may be found throughout Zurich and determining where to stay as a first-time visitor need not be complicated. This guide outlines three neighboring areas to consider booking your lodging. Two of these "areas" are essentially subsets of Zurich's Altstadt or Old Town and the third is adjacent to the Old Town area. In each case, these sections of town provide easy access to main sights, transportation, shopping, and dining.

Other areas are not detailed here simply because they are not as central to the Old Town region of town or close to the train station. In addition, the focus of this guide is on hotels and not apartment rentals such as Air B & B. When considering lodging, using a source such as TripAdvisor.com or Booking.com is recommended as they can provide far more detail and up-to-date reviews.

Recommendation

Good news – this is a large area where you generally can't go wrong.
This sector for lodging stretches from the train station, includes all of Old Town, and some of the right bank area just south of Old Town.

The Three Suggested Lodging Areas:

1 - Train Station and Northern Old Town: All properties are within a few minutes' walk of the train station, and most are in the northern portions of Old Town.

2 - Lower Old Town and Zürich Enge: This area comprises the southern portions of Old Town, down to the lake, along with several quality properties slightly west of the ferry terminal.

3 – Right Shore: This area provides easy access to the lakeshore and Sechselänplatz, a large open park and venue for events. [18]

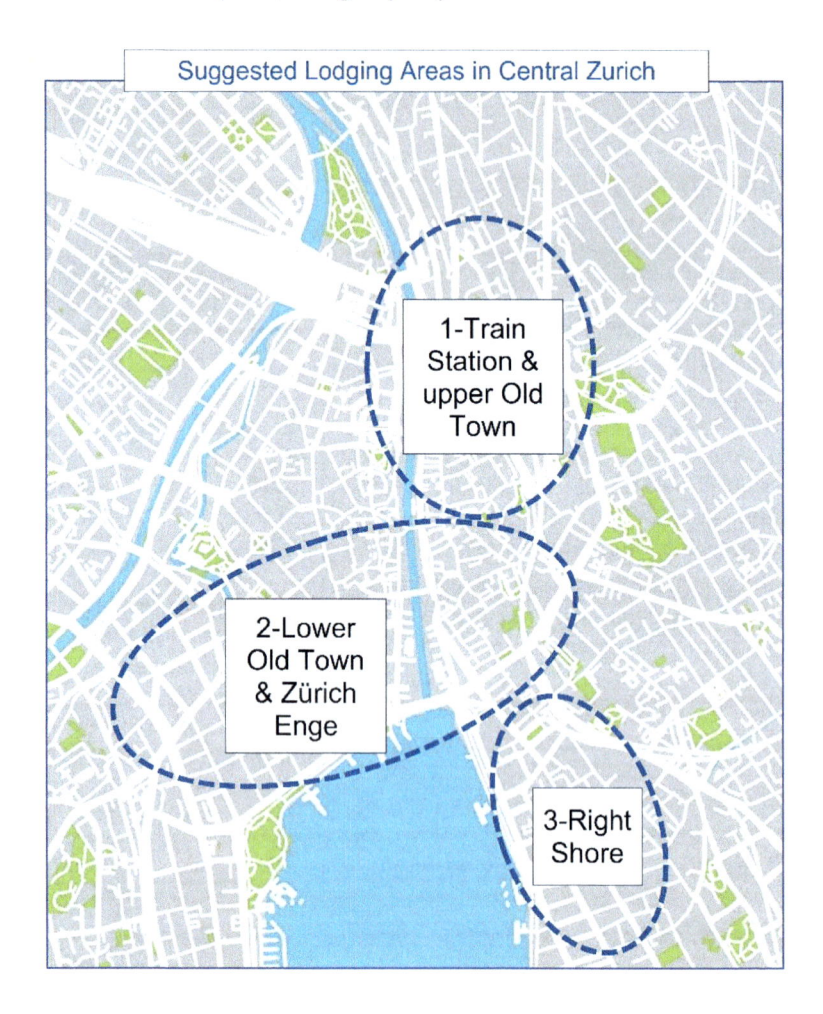

Suggested Lodging Areas in Central Zurich

1-Train Station & upper Old Town

2-Lower Old Town & Zürich Enge

3-Right Shore

---

[18] **Lodging Area Names** – The area names depicted here are not formal Zurich area or neighborhood names. These are used in this chapter simply as a directional aid to help understand where this suggested areas for lodging sit.

The Dolder Grande: Before delving into the list of recommended hotels in central Zurich, there is one hotel/resort which sits slightly outside of the suggested areas for lodging, but it does deserve special mention, *The Dolder Grand Resort & Spa.* While this property is not convenient to the sights of central Zurich or the transportation system, this guidebook would be remiss in not mentioning it as it is somewhat iconic to Zurich, and you can't miss seeing it from the lake.

For starters, this luxury hotel is intended for those with excess wads of cash or crypto currency as you can plan on spending a minimum of CHF 750 a night, and more likely a bit over CHF 950 for a basic room.

The resort which sits on the low hills overlooking the city's Right Shore area is truly beautiful and if you can, do consider it. Oh, bring your golf clubs as well.

For details the website is: www.TheDolderGrand.com

The Dolder Grand Resort & Spa
Photo Source: Whgler - Wikipedia

Now on to the hotels intended for the rest of us. Oh, you may still want to bring a healthy budget. Zurich is expensive.

1-Train Station & Upper Old Town/ Altstadt:[19] Lodging in the heart and northern portions of Old Town. Easy access to just about everything including the train station, small plazas, the river, and more restaurants than you could count. The only negatives are a bit of noise and crowds as this is in the heart of the tourist-centric area.

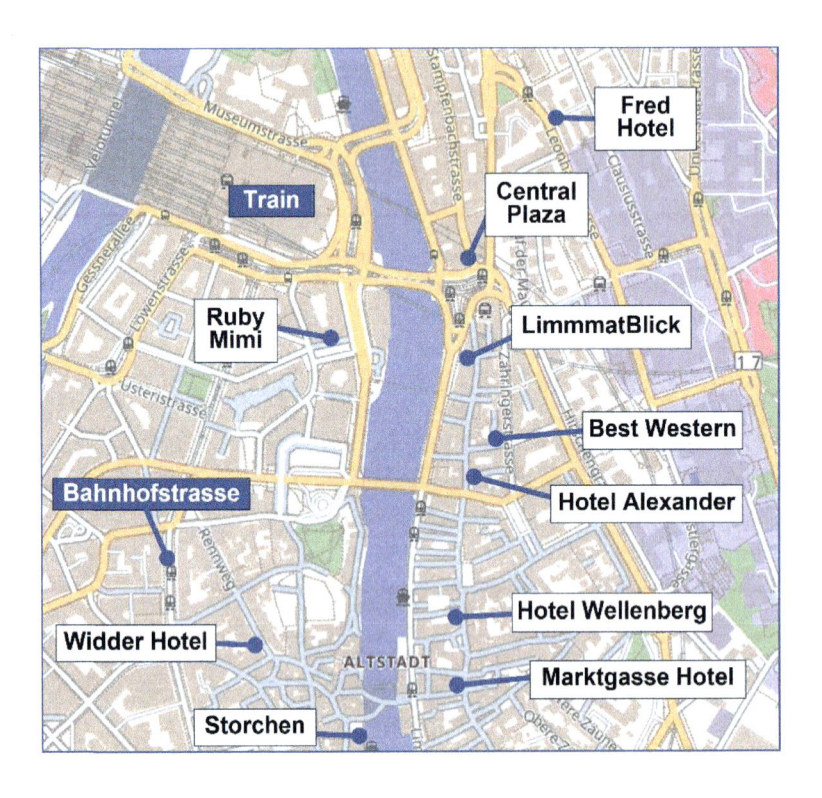

---

[19] **Lodging Ratings in this Guide:** All ratings depicted for hotels in this Starting-Point Guide are a mix of the author's opinion and blend of external rating sources. No one single source was used. As a bit of general advice, consider utilizing your favorite booking source such as Trip Advisor or Hotels.com to see how those services rate each property.

The Central Plaza Hotel faces the river & train station.
Photo Source: Central Plaza Hotel

Properties to consider in **Zurich's Northern Old Town** (Representative Listing Only – Not Every Hotel is Cited Here)		
Hotel Name	**Rating**	**Website**
Best Western Plus Hotel Zürcherhof	3.5	www.Zurcherhof.ch Moderately priced, good quality property.
Central Plaza Hotel	4	www.Central.ch Convenient to the train station. High quality restaurant.
Fred Hotel	3.5	www.FredHotels.ch Moderately priced. Close to train station & university.
Hotel Alexander	3.5	www.Hotel-Alexander.ch Boutique hotel in the heart of Old Town.
LimmatBlick	3	www.Limmatblick.ch River front, boutique hotel.

A Starting-Point Guide

Properties to consider in **Zurich's Northern Old Town**
(Representative Listing Only – Not Every Hotel is Cited Here)

Hotel Name	Rating	Website
Marktgasse Hotel	4	www.MarktGasseHotel.ch Centrally located boutique inn
Ruby Mimi Hotel & Bar	4	www.Ruby-Hotels.com Elegant and contemporary near the train station.
Storchen Zürich Lifestyle Boutique	5	www.Storchen.ch Pure luxury on the river.
Widder Hotel	4.5	www.WidderHotel.com Luxury hotel between the river and the main shopping area.

The Storchen Lifestyle Boutique 5-star river front luxury in one of Switzerland's oldest hotels.
Photo Source: Roland zh - Wikipedia

2-Central to Southern Old Town/Altstadt: This area stretches south from central Old Town, down to the river and, with a few properties near Zurich's 2nd District, the Left Shore area. Some of the suggested hotels are in the Enge area of town and close to the large lakeside arboretum. Several high-end, luxury properties are here.

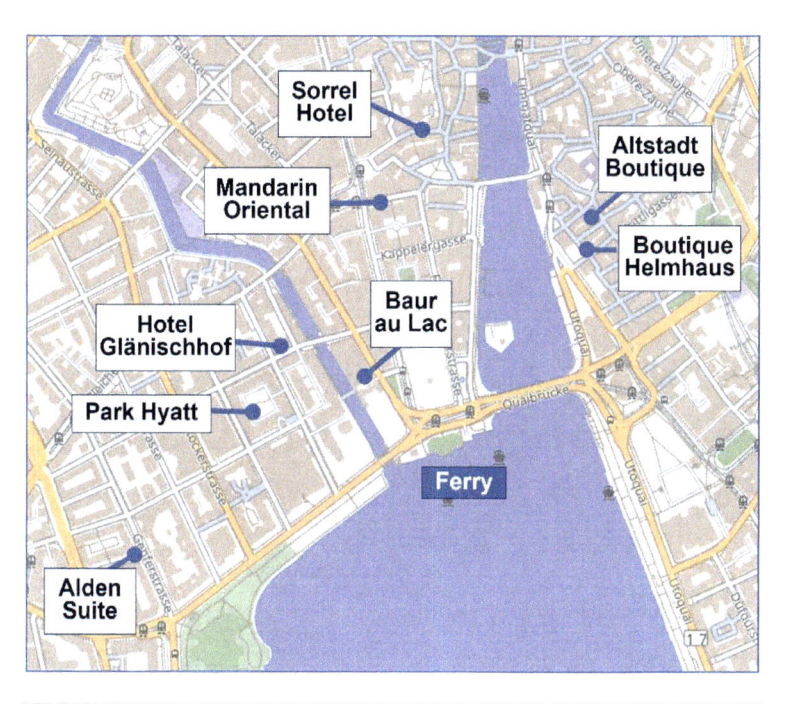

Properties to consider in the **lower Old Town area**
(Representative Listing Only – Not Every Hotel is Cited Here)

Hotel Name	Rating	Website
Alden Suite Hotel Splügenschloss	4.5	www.Leonardo-Hotels.de Luxury in a suburban setting.
Altstadt Boutique Hotel & Bar	3	www.Hotel-Altstadt.ch Quiet, small hotel near the river.

Properties to consider in the **lower Old Town area**
(Representative Listing Only – Not Every Hotel is Cited Here)

Hotel Name	Rating	Website
Baur au Lac	5	www.BaurAuLac.ch Pure luxury. Large grounds, and on a canal near the lake.
Boutique Hotel Helmhaus	4	www.Helmhaus.ch Well-located midsize hotel.
Hotel Glärnischhof by Trinity	4	HotelGlaernischhof.ch Large, full-service, luxury property.
Mandarin Oriental Savoy	4.5	MandarinOriental.com Luxury hotel near shopping and central Old Town
Park Hyatt Hotel	4.5	www.Hyatt.com Large luxury hotel a bit off from central Old Town.
Sorrel Hotel St. Peter	4	www.SorellHotels.com Very central, quality lodging near St. Peter Church.

Baur au Lac Hotel

The Baur au Lac Hotel - pure luxury near central Zurich.
Photo Source: Roland ZH - Wikipedia

3-Right Shore Area: Immediately south of Old Town is an enjoyable area along the Right Bank of Lake Zurich. This is an excellent area for strolling along the lake and enjoying lake activities. Also, there is a large plaza, the Sechseläutenplatz which is frequently used for open markets and major events. Tram lines are readily available here.

Properties to consider in the **Right Shore Area**		
(Representative Listing Only – Not Every Hotel is Cited Here)		
Hotel Name	Rating	Website
Ambassador Hotel	4	www.AmbassadorHotel.ch Close to the lake with views.
AMERON Zürich Bellerive au Lac	4	AmeronCollection.com Lake facing rooms and close to water sports.
Boutique Hotel NI-MO	3.5	www.Hotel-nimo.ch Small hotel close to shopping and dining.

A Starting-Point Guide

Properties to consider in the **Right Shore Area**
(Representative Listing Only – Not Every Hotel is Cited Here)

Hotel Name	Rating	Website
Hotel Europe	4	www.EuropeHotel.ch Convenient mid-size hotel.
Hotel Opera	4	www.OperaHotel.ch Full-service, luxury property.
La Réserve Eden au Lac Zurich	5	LaReserve-Zurich.com Waterfront luxury with multiple restaurants. Pricey.

La Reserve Eden au Lac - **Luxury on the lake.**

7: Points of Interest in Central Zurich

The sights in Zurich include small plazas, quaint shopping areas, swimming parks, and the traditional and expected array of museums. We all have different preferences with some people preferring to spend their time in world-class museums while others are happy to just stroll the town to get a feel for it and perhaps do some people watching in the process. Listed here are a variety of attractions and there should be something here for everyone.

> ### Zurich's Main Attraction is… Zurich
> As with many cities in Europe, the main attraction is the town itself. Yes, there are some marvelous sights, but don't forget to check out this town first by simply strolling around and exploring its avenues and especially the riverfront and lakeshore areas.

The number of sights in Zurich is broad with nearly twenty of them identified here. To help you locate a place of interest, these are organized into three geographical areas with a separate grouping for each area:

- **Central & Old Town / Altstadt:** Points of interest in, or very close to Zurich's Old Town. The area stretches from the train station down to Lake Zurich. Most, but not all, of the attractions cited here are within a reasonable walking distance.
- **Slightly Further Out:** Several popular Zurich destinations require a bit of travel to reach them, but are still within the metropolitan area. This ranges from the zoo to lake and mountain adventures and are cited in the following chapter.

Zurich Points of Interest List

Map #	Name	Type
	**Old Town / Altstadt Area – This Chapter** (Listed in geographic order from north to south)	
1	Swiss National Museum	History & Culture Museum
2	Polybahn	Funicular in Old Town
3	Niederdorf	Old Town – Right Bank
4	Limmatquai	Riverside Promenade
5	Lindenhof	Historic River Overlook
6	Bahnhofstrasse	Shopping Street & Area
7	St. Peter	Church – Left Bank
8	Fraumünster	Church – Left Bank
9	Grossmünster	Church – Right Bank
10	Kunsthaus Zürich	Art Museum
	**A Bit Outside of Central Zurich – See Chapter 8** (Listed geographically)	
11	Zoo Zürich	Zoo & Large Park Area
12	FIFA Museum	Sports Museum
13	Rietberg Museum	Art Museum
14	Quaianlagen	Lakeside Promenade
15	Seebad Utoquai	Swimming & Water Sports
16	Zürichhorn	Lakeside Park – Right Shore
17	Uetilberg	Mountain with Vista Points
18	Felsenegg	Low Mountain with Views
19	Lindt Chocolate	Candy Factory & Museum

Central Zurich Points of Interest

Old Town / Altstadt: Consider starting your explorations at the prominent Lindenhof Overlook and then venturing out from there. This is labeled number 5 on this list and all other district attractions are within an easy walk from here with the greatest distance being down to the lakeshore and ferry port.

This entire area measures roughly 1 mile north-to-south and ½ mile west-to-east. This is an easy area to explore on foot unless you have mobility limitations. Much of the area is flat and having the Limmat River flow through the center adds many enjoyable photo opportunities and places to stroll. Another huge plus here is the limited automobile traffic.

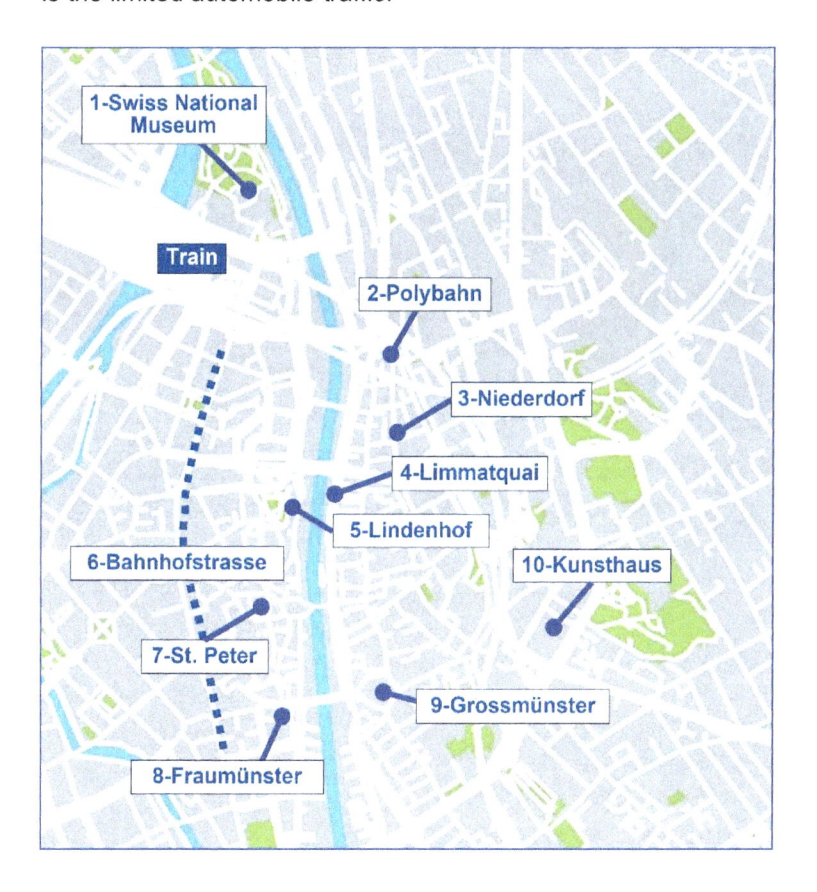

- 1-Swiss National Museum
- Train
- 2-Polybahn
- 3-Niederdorf
- 4-Limmatquai
- 5-Lindenhof
- 6-Bahnhofstrasse
- 10-Kunsthaus
- 7-St. Peter
- 9-Grossmünster
- 8-Fraumünster

1 – Swiss National Museum / Landesmuseum Zürich: Adjacent to Zurich's main train station and numerous tram lines is the massive Landesmuseum. This museum complex could easily take a full day to explore as there are several separate areas including but not limited to:

- History of Switzerland
- Archaeology in Switzerland
- Culture of Switzerland
- Textiles and Clothing
- Ceramics of Switzerland

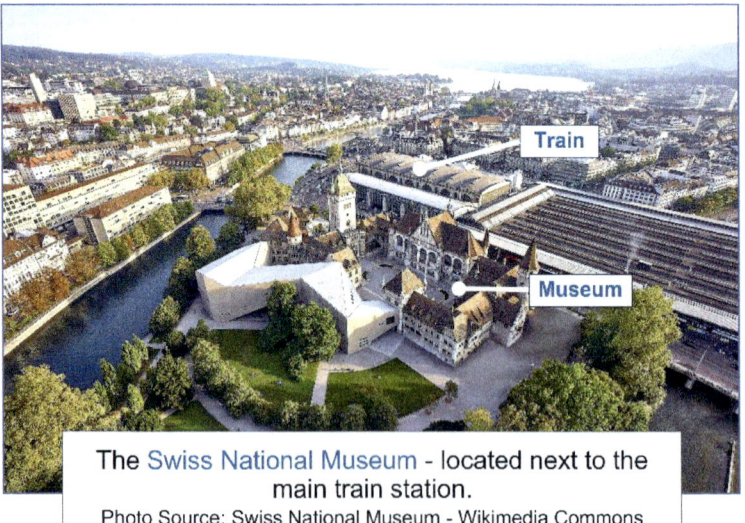

The Swiss National Museum - located next to the main train station.
Photo Source: Swiss National Museum - Wikimedia Commons

Facilities: A bistro and boutique are on the property. Also, there is a large park just north of the museum which connects it to the confluence of the Limmat and Sihl Rivers.

Website: www.LandesMuseum.ch

Hours: Closed Monday. Most days it is open from 10AM until 5 or 7PM, depending on the day.

2 – Polybahn / UBS Polybahn: An enjoyable, but short, funicular in central Zurich. This ride only goes about 2 blocks and lasts just four minutes, but it is a fun way to explore a section of Zurich. The route travels from Central Square in Old Town up to the ETH Technical University. Albert Einstein graduated from here.

The UBS Polybahn funicular
Photo Source: MOs810 - Wikimedia Commons

Once you are at the top, there is a large open plaza with a restaurant. The location provides some good views over the heart of Zurich. (Moderate views given the small rise in elevation, but still some pretty good views.) This funicular has been in operation since 1889 and takes you up 134 feet. (41 meters)

There is a small cost, but this is included in the Zurich Card and local ZVV transportation passes.

~ ~ ~ ~ ~ ~

3 – Niederdorf / Old Town: The term "Niederdorf" means low village in German. This right-bank sector is often considered to be the heart of Zurich's Old Town. This is a pedestrian zone so, given the minimal auto traffic, you can stroll in peace and enjoy one of the many outdoor cafes. The biggest plus to this area are the many appealing narrow lanes and historic buildings. There are also a few small plazas such as the attractive Hirschenplatz.

A Starting-Point Guide

One of many attractive lanes in the Niederdorf area.

This section of town is bordered by the busy Central Plaza on the north and the Limmatquai promenade along the river. Near the southern portion of this area is the Grossmünster Church and the attractive Rathaus. (Rathaus is the town hall in German cities).

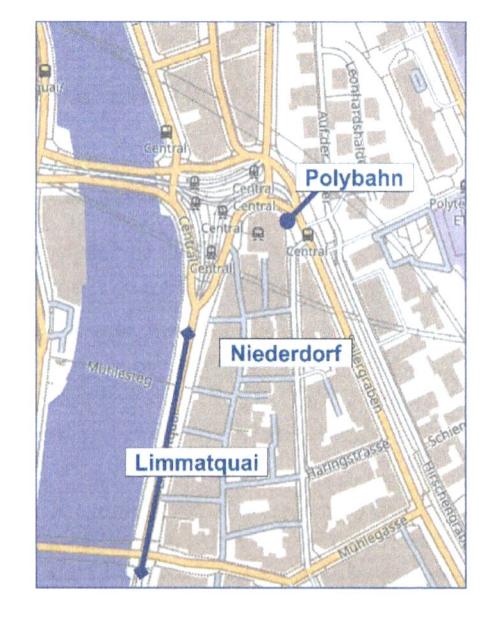

~ ~ ~ ~ ~ ~

4 – Limmatquai: This nearly 1 mile long (1.6 km) boulevard runs alongside the Limmat River on the river's right bank. This thoroughfare is often cited as Zurich's most appealing lane. While there are trams running along here, this is still part of Zurich's pedestrian area. Come here for great photo opportunities, river-facing cafes, and even boat rentals. This popular lane connects the Central Plaza which is near the train station down to the lake.

The Limmatquai riverside boulevard.
Photo Source: Roland zh - Wikimedia Commons

Tram running along the Limmatquai.

5 – Lindenhof Park & Overlook: This is a small park which sits above the Limmat River on the left bank and on the site of a former Roman settlement. It is one of the best sites in central Zurich to get a good overall view of the old town, the river, the Limmatquai Boulevard, and the lush green hills which frame the city. One caution, if you approach this from the river, it is a steep walk uphill to reach the park and overlook.

The Lindenhof Overlook sits above the river providing excellent views.
Photo Source: Perconte - Wikimedia Commons

The Lindenhof Overlook Park
Photo Source: A Praefcke - Wikimedia Commons

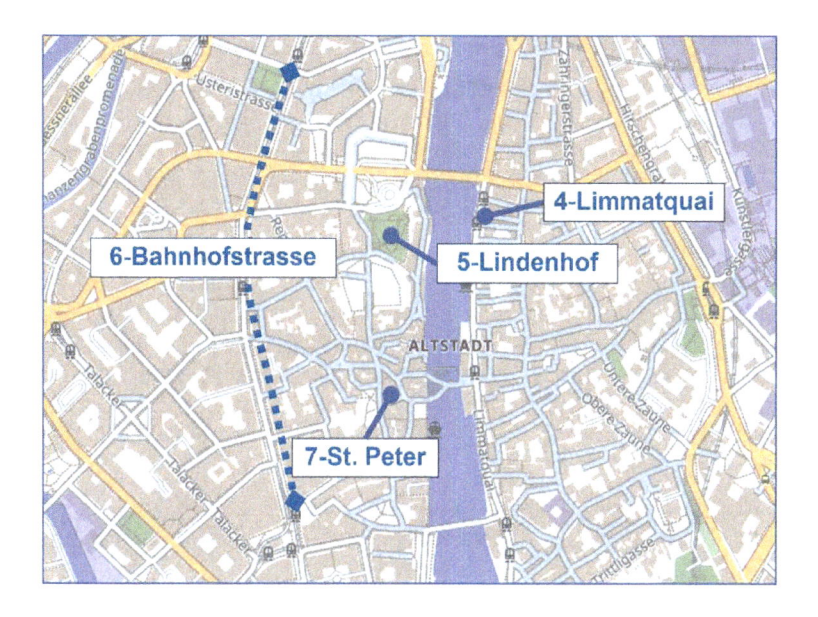

6 – Bahnhofstrasse: Zurich's premier shopping street and district. This three-quarter mile long street is known as one of Europe's and the world's most expensive shopping districts. Come here for a dazzling variety of upscale boutiques and many restaurants.

The street sits just a few blocks west of the river and runs from the train station at the north to the lake at its southern end.

Note: shops are generally closed on Sunday.

The Bahnhofstrasse
One of Europe's most expensive shopping streets.
Photo Source: Roland ZH - Wikipedia

7 – St. Peter Church: This is one of Zurich's main central churches. It is in the Lindenhof area of town, close to the river and the Lindenhof overlook. This is a "reformed/Protestant" church, which was established under the Calvinist religious movement. The current structure was opened in 1706 and was the first Protestant church in the region.

A hard to miss feature of this church is the tall steeple with its large clock. Today it is largely known for its huge clockface, which is the largest in Europe. One interesting aspect of this church tower is it was used as a fire watch tower up until 1911. This function led to an interesting dual ownership of the building which is even in place today. Two entities own various parts of the building with the city owning the tower and the main building and the nave, owned by the church.

Today, guided tours are available and group tours up into the tower are available. Check the church website for details and fees.

Church Website: www.St-Peter-zh.ch

St. Peter Church
Photo Source: Joseolgon - Wikimedia Commons

8 – Fraumünster Church: This "Church of our Lady" or "Women's Church" is built on the site of what had been an abbey. It has a history dating back to 853AD although little of the original structure remains. The current structure is built in the Gothic style and is an active parish church.

> This is formally a
> "Cultural Property of National Significance"
> for Switzerland

There are many interesting features here and this church is well worth a visit. Tours are available and there is a gift shop on site. Some of the more noteworthy aspects of this church include:

Photo Source: Juerg-hug
Wikimedia Commons

- Marc Chagall windows. There are five tall stained-glass windows by this artist which were installed in 1970. Each window depicts a different biblical story.
- Crypt Museum: In 2016, the crypt under the abbey was opened and made public. This area dates to the 9th century and several holy relics are held here. Tours of the crypt are available.
- Organ: There is a huge pipe organ with 5,793 pipes.

Church Website: www.Fraumuenster.ch

A Starting-Point Guide

~ ~ ~ ~ ~ ~

9 – Grossmünster Church: Directly across the river from the Fraumünster church is the Grossmünster Church. This tall Protestant church is a former monestary.

The Grossmünster Church
Overlooking the Limmat River
Photo Source: Aak47 - Wikipedia

This church is where the Swiss-German Reformation began. It was constructed between 1100 and 1220. Among the highlights are stained-glass windows, a Romanesque crypt, and an attractive cloister garden. Towering over the church are twin towers which are a visible landmark that can be seen for miles around. Visitors may go to the top of one of the towers for great views. Caution, there is no elevator and you need to climb over 180 stairs to reach the top.

Hours: Visitor hours vary by the season. In general, you can count on it being open to tour from 10AM to 5PM.

Fees: There is a small fee to tour the interior, the crypt, and climb up the tower, the Karlstrum.

Website: www.GrossMuenster.ch

~ ~ ~ ~ ~ ~

10 – Kunsthaus Zürich: This is Switzerland's largest art museum in size and 2nd in the breadth of its collections. This expansive facility sits on the edge of Zurich's Old Town and is roughly a 7- to-8-minute walk from the river.

The Kunsthaus Art Museum
Photo Source: Roland zh - Wikipedia

The collections span over 800 years of art and include items from the Middel Ages up to current time. Notable artists such as Edvard Munch, Picasso, Claude Monet, and van Gogh are represented here. The largest focus is on Swiss art as this is how the museum's collections began.

There is over 13,000 square meters (10,800 sq feet) of exhibit space across numerous galleries, so it can take some time to visit the major permanent exhibits.

There is also a café and gift shop onsite.

A work by Henri Rousseau in the Kunsthaus.

Hours: Closed on Monday. Most days it is open from 10AM to 6PM.

Website: www.Kunsthaus.ch

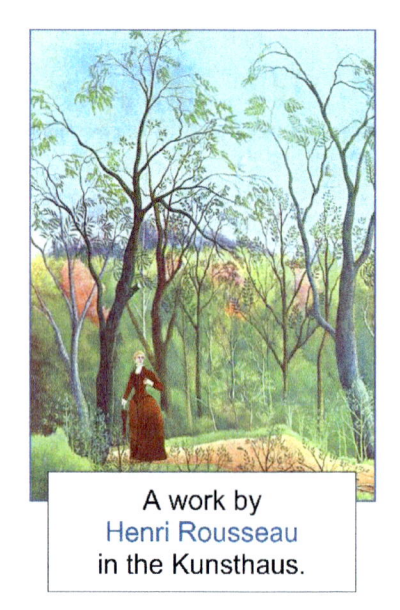

8: Points of Interest – Slightly Further Out

In addition to the attractions in central Zurich which were cited in the previous chapter, there are several notable destinations just a short distance from the city center. This selection of points of interest provides a good cross section of what is available on Zurich's outskirts. It does not list every opportunity for fun, especially when it comes to outdoor activities.

What is here is a delightful mix ranging from a candy factory to low mountain adventures and every destination is reachable by Zurich's tram and train system.

\multicolumn{3}{c}{**Points of Interest A Bit Outside of Central Zurich**}		
Map #	**Name**	**Type**
\multicolumn{3}{c}{Listed Geographically – from North to South[20]}		
11	Zoo Zürich	Zoo & Large Park Area
12	FIFA Museum	Sports Museum
13	Rietberg Museum	Art Museum
14	Quaianlagen	Lakeside Promenade
15	Seebad Water Parks	Swimming & Water Sports

---

[20] **Attraction Numbering:** This list starts with #11 due simply to the fact that the list of attractions cited in the previous chapter ended with #10.

A Starting-Point Guide

Points of Interest A Bit Outside of Central Zurich

Map #	Name	Type
16	Zürichhorn	Lakeside Park – Right Shore
17	Uetilberg	Mountain with Vista Points
18	Felsenegg	Low Mountain with Views
19	Lindt Chocolate	Candy Factory & Museum

11 – Zoo Zürich & Park Area: The Zürich Zoologischer Garten is about 1.5 miles northeast of the center of town. This is one of Europe's largest and oldest zoos. It opened in 1929 and has over 300 different species available to view. In 2020, the size of the zoo grew in size to the current 67 acres (27 hectares). It evolved into a facility which focuses as much on the differing eco systems as it does on the animals.

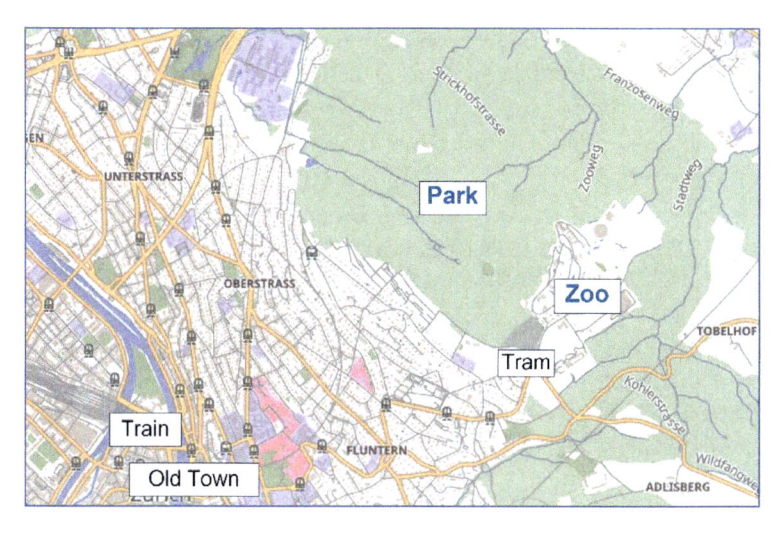

The zoo is open all year, but hours do vary slightly with the season. Typical opening hours are 9AM and close at 5 or 6PM.

Adjacent to the zoo is a large state park, the ***Escherhöle Park***. This park covers a hilly area and is a perfect escape for hiking, biking, and even horse riding.

Both the park and the zoo can be reached by city tram or bus. The tram stop is about a five-minute walk to the zoo entrance or, if you prefer to do some hiking, some trails into the park start a short distance from here.

Website and Apps: The zoo's website is www.Zoo.ch. Then, you may download a detailed zoo app from this site. If you wish details on the trails inside the neighboring park, consider downloading the Komoot app. This is an excellent app to use for hiking almost anywhere, including this park.

12 – FIFA Museum: The worldwide headquarters for FIFA (Soccer in America and Football for the rest of the world) is in Zurich. While the headquarters is not a tourist attraction, this organization has crafted a superb ultra-modern museum to honor the sport. This is more than a museum, it is also a set of interactive experiences. So, if you are interested in soccer, this should be high on your list of spots to visit. There are three floors of exhibits which cover the history and highlights of the sport.

Hours: Closed on Monday. Other days, open from 10AM to 6PM

Location: First, do not head to the FIFA headquarters. This museum is just a short distance southwest from Old Town while the FIFA headquarters is across town, northeast of Old Town and close to the zoo. The museum is located in the Enge neighborhood.

Transportation to Here: The museum is across the street from Zurich Enge train station. This is a busy station, but not Zurich's main station.

Website: www.FifaMuseum.com

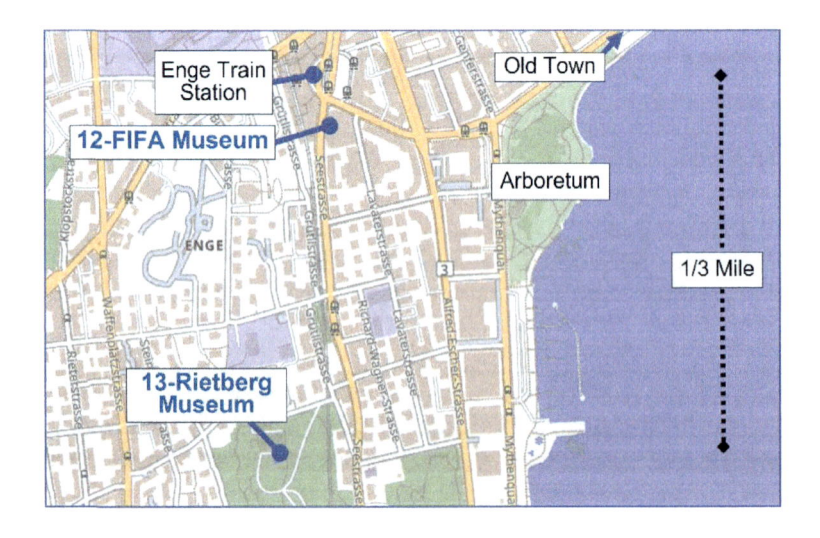

13 – Museum Rietberg: This is one of two art museums outlined in this guide. The other, and much larger, is the Kunsthaus, which is listed in the previous chapter. The Museum Rietberg's focus is on art from Asia, Africa, and Oceania.

Located in a set of former villas, there is a grand atmosphere to this museum and its setting. The complex includes several buildings which all are former villas in a park setting. The facilities go beyond just the three connected villas, there are also underground exhibits.

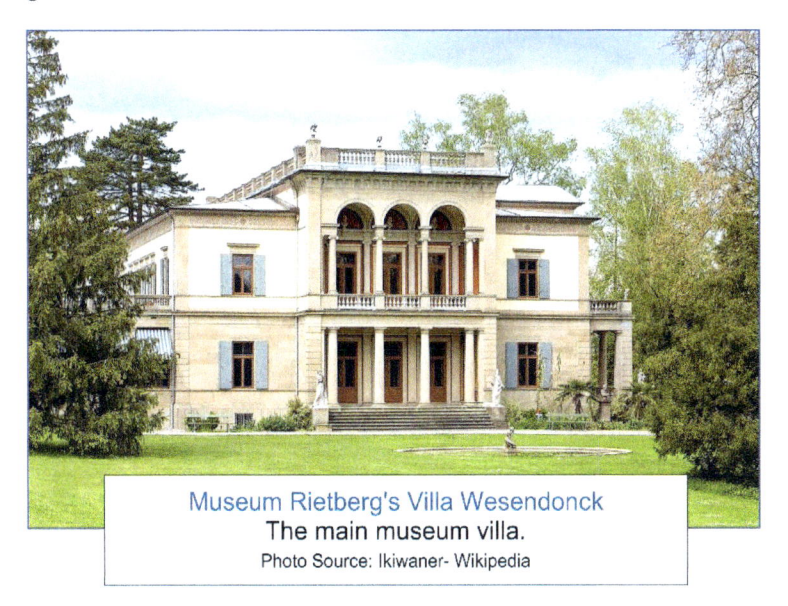

Museum Rietberg's Villa Wesendonck
The main museum villa.
Photo Source: Ikiwaner- Wikipedia

Hours: Closed on Monday. Other days its open from 10AM to 5PM.

Getting Here: Take bus # 7 to the Museum Reitberg stop or walk two blocks south from the Zürich Enge train station. If you prefer, this is a pleasant five-minute walk over to the lakeshore.

Website: www.Rietberg.ch

Waterfront Fun:

The three points of interest which follow offer opportunities to appreciate and play at the lakefront in the Right Shore area.

These attractions are within an easy walk of each other or, if you prefer, accessible by tram. These locations include two waterfront parks and a water sports area. This is in addition to the adjacent marinas and boat rental opportunities.

~ ~ ~ ~ ~ ~

14 – Quaianlagen Utoquai: For starters, the term Quainanlagen essentially means "lakeshore sites." There are lakeside areas and parks on both sides of the lake. On the right shore area is a series of connected parks which are lined with marinas, boat rentals, a small ferry terminal, and even areas for swimming. If you wanted, you could stroll both sides of the lake along these promenades which spans six kilometers.

The Utoquai portion of this extended park was built in 1887. It is tree lined which provides for enjoyable shaded walks. It is a favorite area for locals and visitors alike to take in the ambiance of this beautiful lake with views of the Enge section of the city across the lake and mountains in the distance. There are many long benches to relax and enjoy a warm day and no shortage of food stalls.

Central Zurich Points of Interest

Quaianlagen Utoquai - Waterfront Promenade
Photo Source: Google Maps

View from Quaianlagen of the Left Shore / Enge Area of Zurich with the Alps in the background.
Photo Source: Roland ZH- Wikimedia Commons

15 – Seebad Utoquai & Other Water Sports: One of the attractions alongside the Quainanlagen promenade is a waterpark of sorts, the Seebad Utoquai. There is a similar facility across the lake, the Seebad Enge. Either of these sites are great ways to enjoy the lake on a sunny day including swimming pools, sunbathing areas, diving boards, swim platforms, and there is even a snack bar. Restrooms and changing rooms are on site. There is a small fee to visit here and reservations are not required.

The Seebad Utoquai Floating Water Sports Park

Adjacent to this floating water sports facility are two boat rental docks. In each case, you have options of renting a variety of craft including:
- Peddle boats
- Paddle boards
- Sail boats
- Small power boats

Websites for the boat rental sites are:
www.Lago-Zuerich.ch and www.BootsVermietung-Seefeld.ch

~ ~ ~ ~ ~ ~

16 – Zürichhorn & Chinese Garden: At the southern end of Zurich's Quainanlagen promenade, is a large park which spans roughly 50 acres (20 hectares).

In addition to the expansive green spaces, one of the more notable features here is the Chinese Garden. This park is one of the largest Chinese gardens outside of mainland China. It includes large sculpture gardens and koi ponds. There is a small fee to enter the Chinese Gardens, but not the Zürichhorn park.

The park portion of Zürichhorn includes several opportunities for fun and relaxation.

- Large open green spaces
- Waterside restaurant
- Water Taxi terminal. You can catch rides from here up the Limmat river or to several locations across the lake.
- Areas to swim and sunbathe
- A pavilion designed by the famed architect Le Corbusier.

Zürichhorn Park
Photo Source: Roland ZH- Wikimedia Commons

~ ~ ~ ~ ~ ~

17 – Uetilberg Mountain: Often cited as a "mountain," Uetilberg is actually more of a tall hill which provides great opportunities for viewing Zurich, Lake Zurich, and the Alps to the south. It sits in the low Albis chain of mountains which includes Felsenegg to the south.

Uetilberg Lookout Tower
Photo Source: K Spalinger-Roes Wikimedia Commons

Central Zurich Points of Interest

Uetilberg stands 2,850 feet (869 meters) in altitude, or almost exactly 2,000 feet above Lake Zurich. At the crest you will find:
- Restaurant and small hotel
- Railway station (A few feet below the summit)
- Numerous trails for hiking and mountain biking. (Some are steep)
- Observation tower which provides another 236 feet (72 meters) of elevation for increased viewing. There is a small fee to climb it. (No elevator)

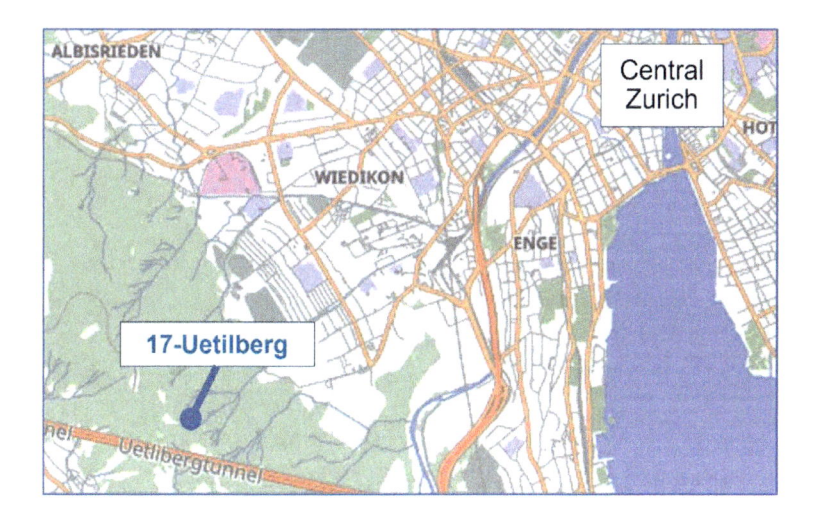

Getting Here: Travel time by public transportation from central Zurich is roughly 45 minutes. This includes an enjoyable train ride, followed by a ten-minute walk from the station up to the tower, overlook, and restaurants. A suggested route is to depart from Zurich's main train station and catch the Uetilberg train. This is about a 25-minute ride. From the station, there is an uphill stroll up to the crest.

Website: Go to www.Zuerich.com then to the page on Uetilberg.

~ ~ ~ ~ ~ ~

A Starting-Point Guide

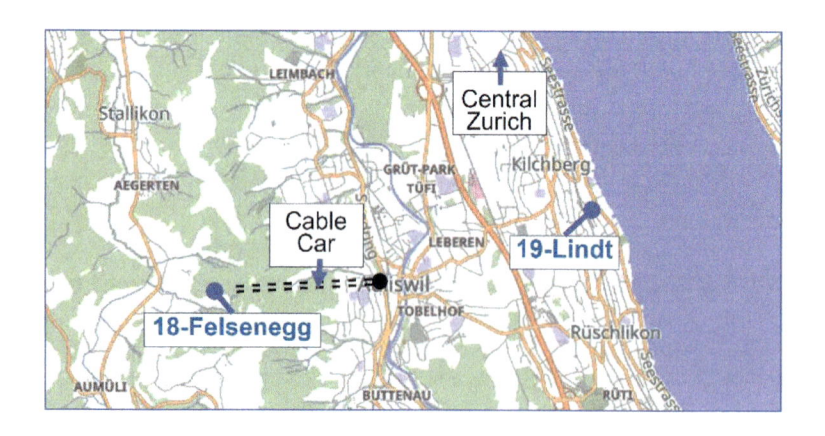

18 – Felsenegg Mountain: A short distance south of Uetilberg is another low mountain (or tall hill) with excellent views. Felsenegg rises to 2638 feet (800 meters), so it is almost as tall as Uetilberg. This easy to reach viewpoint also has a pleasant array of amenities including a café, overlooks, and numerous hiking trails. There is even a trail which connects to Uetilberg if you have a full day available.

A fun aspect of this destination is the ride up via a local cable car, the "Adliswil-Felsenegg AG." It is so named because its base is in the village of Felsenegg.

The Adliswil-Felsenegg Cable Car

Getting Here: Take the train from central Zurich to the Adliswil station. From there, it is a ten-minute walk, slightly uphill, to the cable car station.

Website: www.Felsenegg.com

19 – Lindt Home of Chocolates: This enjoyable and interactive museum sits close to Lake Zurich in the small town of Kilchberg. This is a mix of a chocolate factory, a museum and, of course, one heck of a large candy store.

A notable feature here is the tall chocolate fountain which pours chocolate from a height of 9 meters. Then you can go through several interactive exhibits which even include a course on chocolate making. Advance purchase of tickets is highly advised as this is a popular destination.

A cafe is on site to help round out your diet while you are here.

The Lindt Home Of Chocolate Museum
Photo Source: Lindt-Home-Of-Chocolates.com

Getting to Here: If you travel by ferry or train, the journey from central Zurich will take between 20 to 30 minutes. In each case, there will be about a 10-minute walk from either the Bürkliplatz boat terminal or the Kilchberg train station.

Website: www.Lindt-Home-of-Chocolate.com

9: Lake Zurich, Ferries, & Boat Tours

Lake Zurich:[21] Stretching for 25 miles (40 km) in a southeasterly direction from central Zurich, the lake is lined with a scenic variety of: low hills, towns and villages; marinas; and even vineyards. As you might expect, very little of the shoreline is undeveloped, especially in the upper portions near Zurich.

Lake Zurich - Viewed from Felsenegg Mountain
Photo Source: Roland zh - Wikimedia Commons

---

[21] Lake Name in German: *Zürichsee*

A few additional facts about Lake Zurich:

- This is a narrow lake. At its widest, it is just two miles (3 km) across.
- The average depth is notable at 161 feet (49 meters). At its deepest point, it is 446 feet or 136 meters deep.
- Different names are used to indicate the sector of the lake. The name *Zürichsee* is often used to describe the area closest to Zurich. The name *Obersee* is used to define the southern area furthest from the city.
- Portions of the lake may be found in three different Swiss cantons. (A canton is similar to a U.S State or Canadian Province).
- The lake can, and does, freeze on occasion.
- Not one large river forms this lake, but numerous streams and small rivers feed into it.

Ferries & Traveling on Them: For many of us, spending part of a day exploring an area by ferry or tour boat can be just plain fun. With Lake Zurich, you have many options to travel the lake on the ferry system ranging from a simple water taxi transit to dinner excursions.

The Lake Zurich Ferry Fleet offers an enjoyable variety of vessels ranging from classic to modern.

A Starting-Point Guide

Ferry Ports & Towns Along Lake Zurich: There are over thirty ports along the lake, providing substantial opportunities to visit area towns and villages.

A word of caution about what you will encounter at most ferry stops and towns along the lake. These stops are generally geared to local citizens and not tourism. As a result, what you will find in the towns is a blend of a pleasant waterfront community, homes, maybe a restaurant or two, and little more. Still, it can be educational to stop in one of

The ferry service, **ZSG**, is associated with the overall Zurich transportation network of **ZVV**. This enables you to plan trips which utilize both ground and water transportation and purchase combined tickets and passes.

Many ferry stops have train stations within walking distance.

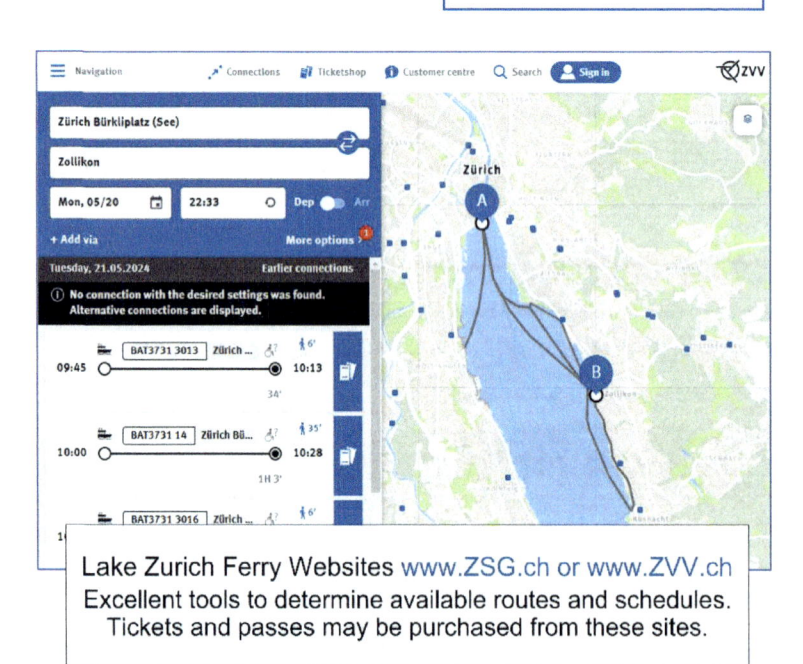

Lake Zurich Ferry Websites www.ZSG.ch or www.ZVV.ch
Excellent tools to determine available routes and schedules.
Tickets and passes may be purchased from these sites.

these towns to gain an understanding of what life is like along the shores of Lake Zurich.

> **Good News**
>
> If you have a Swiss Travel Pass or a Zurich Card, many ferry services may be used at no additional fee.

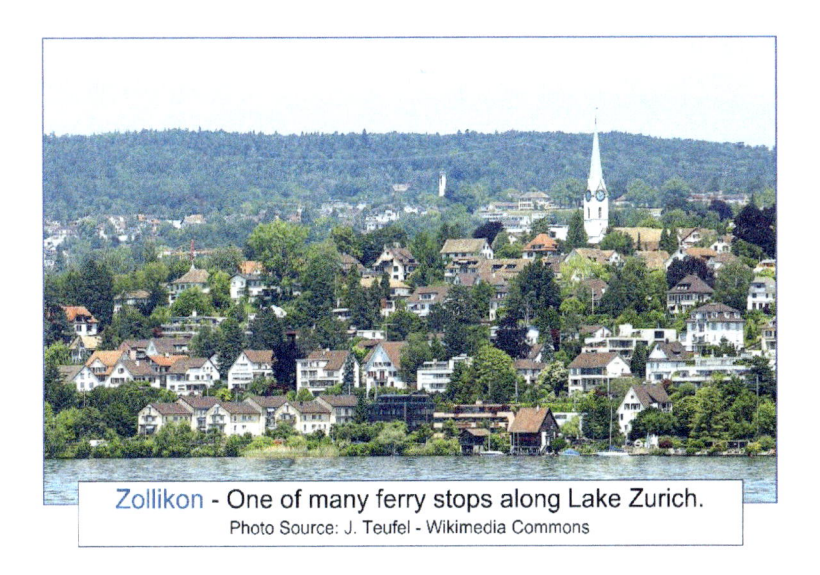

Zollikon - One of many ferry stops along Lake Zurich.
Photo Source: J. Teufel - Wikimedia Commons

Water Taxis: In addition to the ferry system which services Zurich, there are also companies which provide water taxi service. The leading firm, ***Water Taxi Zurich***, operates in a manner similar to an Uber taxi in which owners of their own boats will be on call to take you for a journey on the lake.

In most cases, you will need to reserve your water taxi in advance, just as you would if you were using an Uber.

- Water Taxi Zurich – www.Wassertaxi.ch

Lake Cruises: For most of us, simply spending some time on the lake without having to worry about heading to a particular destination is all that is wanted. The leading firm for this is also ZSG, (www.ZSG.com) and many options are offered ranging from short

lake cruises to specialty food cruises. Some of these enjoyable jaunts include:
- Brunch cruise
- Burger cruise
- Fondue cruise (Okay, this is Switzerland, so fondue it is!)
- Japanese Cuisine cruises
- Murder Mystery Cruises
- Wine cruises
- And many more.

10: Easy Day Trips from Zurich
Natural Wonders & Quaint Towns

Several opportunities for enjoyable and informative day trips out of town are available. These trips range from climbing a mountain to visiting nearby historic and charming cities.

Seven destinations are highlighted here. Given all there is too see in central Switzerland, this is far from being a complete list. However, it does provide a great cross section. Most of these locations are easily reached by the local train system and, with one

A Starting-Point Guide

exception, they are all reachable in 90 minutes or less from central Zurich. The goal is to enable you to have an easy day trip or half-day trip without wearing yourself down.

Day Trip Destinations Included in This Guide [22]		
Name	Distance[23]	Type of Destination
Liechtenstein	50 Miles 80 KM	Europe's 4th smallest country Capital city is Vaduz.
Lucerne	25 Miles 40 KM	Historic and beautiful lakeside city with numerous attractions.
Mt. Pilatus	30 Miles 48 KM	Easy to reach Mountain Adventure adjacent to Lucerne.
Mt. Rigi	23 Miles 37 KM	Low mountain resort area overlooking Lake Lucerne.
Mt. Titlis	43 Miles 69 KM	High mountain adventure in the Alps.
Rhine Falls	21 Miles 34 KM	Beautiful array of waterfalls near the border with Germany.
St. Gallen	39 Miles 63 KM	Small city with historic Old Town area.

---

[22] **Destinations Listed Alphabetically:** The day trip destinations outlined here are organized alphabetically. This order does not suggest any sort of priority or importance in which destination to consider over others.

[23] **Distances Cited:** All distances listed in the table on this page are "as the crow flies" from central Zurich to the center of the destination site or area. Actual driving or train distances will likely be greater.

Tours From Zurich: Before delving into the details on the seven suggested day trips outlined in this guide, it is worth noting that some will require some advance travel planning or even renting a car to reach them. With this in mind, you may want to utilize the resources of one of the tour companies which operate out of Zurich. These firms will take you directly to the destination and reduce most to all of the travel planning hassle. One caution, in some cases, only private tours are available, which can be rather expensive.

Tour Operators:[24] The following firms offer tours to these locations.

- Swiss Day Tours – www.SwissDayTours.com
- Switzerland Tours – www.Switzerland-Tour.com
- Viator – www.Viator.com
- Get Your Guide – www.GetYourGuide.com

Notes on Tours to The Suggested Day Trip Destinations	
Location	**Notes**
Liechtenstein	• A limited number of group & private tours are available, and most tours will include other stops along the way. • Without joining a tour, it is best to rent a car to visit here.
Lucerne and/or Mt Pilatus	• Many tours to Lucerne and Mt. Pilatus are available ranging from half day to full day and there is a good mix of private and group offerings. • Given the ease of traveling here by train and bus from Zurich, unless you have special

---

[24] **Tour Operators Listed:** This is a representative sample of tour providers in the area only and does not include every quality tour service available.

A Starting-Point Guide

Notes on Tours to The Suggested Day Trip Destinations

Location	Notes
	needs, there really isn't much reason to join a tour.
Mt. Rigi	• Tours are available to Mt. Rigi, but are not needed as it is easy to take the train here. The biggest exception is, if you wish to combine a visit to Mt Rigi with Lucerne, a tour bus can reduce overall travel time and hassle to combine the two.
Rhine Falls	• Numerous full-day and half-day tours to the falls and surrounding area are available. Some tours combine a visit to Liechtenstein or St. Gallen. • Train travel to the falls is easy if you do not want to take a tour.
Mt. Titlis	• Tours to Mt. Titlis do offer a good level of convenience and reduction in travel hassle. Many tours also include a visit to Lucerne. • If you prefer to do your own planning, train travel is best, but note that you must change trains in Lucerne. • This is the furthest in travel time of the seven locations listed in this chapter.
St. Gallen	• Many tours are available to St. Gallen, and several include one or both of Liechtenstein or Rhine Falls. • It is easy, however, to travel by train or rental car to this beautiful town. so a tour is not needed.

Liechtenstein and the Capital of Vaduz: To be brutally honest, there is not a lot to do when visiting here. But don't let that keep you from coming. At the very least, it is fun to say that you have visited this small country and have explored its capital city of Vaduz. This capital is small but impressive in the overall quality of buildings and general feel of cleanliness and wealth. It can be helpful to note in advance that the general feel of this small city is very modern, so don't expect a quaint little town.

> **Fun Souvenir**
> You can get a Liechtenstein stamp in your passport at the Tourist Office in Vaduz. There is a small fee to do so.

Map Source: UN Office for Coordination of Humanitarian Affairs & Wikipedia

Vaduz - The Capital of Liechtenstein
Photo Source: St9191-Wikipedia

Some Small Facts About Liechtenstein:

- This is the 4th smallest country in Europe geographically. The three smaller countries are: Vatican City, Monaco, and San Marino.

- The total size of Liechtenstein is 62 square miles (160 sq km) which is roughly the same size as Washington DC. It is 15 miles in length from north to south.

- The population is only 37,900 people (unless someone has had a baby since this was written). The largest city is not the capital of Vaduz, but rather the town of Schaan which is slightly north of Vaduz.

- This country does not have an airport, but it does have a small university with 800 students.

- Liechtenstein has the second highest wealth per capita. Only Monaco ranks higher.

- This is a principality which was first established as part of the Holy Roman Empire in 1719 and later became a sovereign state in 1806. The current prince is Hans-Adam II and he resides in Vaduz Castle which overlooks that town. (So… while it is tempting, don't try to go into the palace to visit although you can hike up to it.)
- The official currency is the Swiss Franc, but your Euros are happily accepted here. (By the way, many of those Swiss Francs are held by the prince as his wealth is estimated to be over 6 billion… so, with no airport, where does he park his private jet?)

What to See and Do in Vaduz: There are some notable museums to explore in the heart of Vaduz in addition to simply enjoying one of the many enjoyable restaurants in the heart of town.

- The Tourist Center: In the heart of this modern town is a large Tourist Center. Come here to get your passport stamped and learn about this country.
- Treasure Chamber: A great way to learn about Liechtenstein. This museum houses art and other treasures held by the royal family during the past 400 years.
- Kunstmuseum Liechtenstein: A large, modern art museum in the heart of Vaduz.
- Liechtenstein National Museum: A former inn which now focuses on the country's history.

How to Get Here: The easiest way to reach this country and its capital is either to drive or join a tour. If you drive, the journey takes slightly over 1 hour each way. You can reach Vaduz and Schann by a mix of train and bus, but this is not advised as it can be very time-consuming to do so.

Websites:
- Country: www.Liechtenstein.li
- Tourist Office: www.Tourismus.li

A Starting-Point Guide

Lucerne: It would be an understatement to say that Lucerne is a popular destination. It is a haven for tourists from around the world for many reasons. For starters, this is an attractive town which is easy to explore on foot. Then, there are numerous and varied attractions near one another which are walkable.

First though, one caution is in order. Lucerne can be crowded, especially during the summer months. So, if you are crowd-averse, then this may not be the destination for you.

Lucerne is easy to combine with a visit to the neighboring Mt. Pilatus although doing so will necessitate that you don't see everything which central Lucerne has to offer.

If you travel here by train, you are in for a treat as this station couldn't be better located. Just step out from the front of Lucerne's train station and the lake is right there. Then, it is a simple matter to walk two blocks over to the famous Chapel Bridge and then across into Old Town.

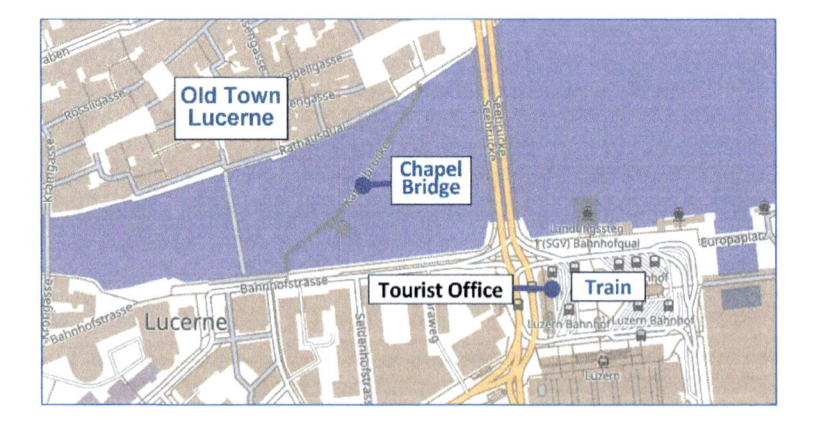

Lucene - Starting-Point Guide
Consider acquiring this additional Starting-Point Guide before your travels.

106

Central Lucerne

Some Facts About Lucerne:
- The German name for this town is Luzern.
- The city population is 82,000 making it the largest city in central Switzerland. The population for the entire metropolitan area is over 220,000.

The Chapel Bridge in central Lucerne

- This is a compact city, and it is easy to explore on foot for most individuals.
- Mark Twain visited here twice.
- Chapel Bridge, or "Kapellbrücke" is the world's oldest covered bridge. This bridge spans the Reuss River which divides Lucerne into two halves.
- This was once a walled city. The Museggmauer wall built in the 14th century was designed to protect the city from attackers. Today, parts of the wall still exist along with four of the original towers.
- During the French Revolution, hundreds of Swiss Guards were massacred. Today, an impressive monument, the *"Lion of Lucerne"* honors them.

Lucerne

The Lucerne Travel Guide App is one of several which can be quite helpful.

Some Leading Points of Interest: There is no shortage of interesting sights here. At the top of the list, is the city itself and its incredible setting adjacent to Lake Lucerne with tall mountains looking down on you. If you do nothing more than simply stroll through the heart of this town and perhaps enjoy a meal or fondue alongside the river, you will come out a winner.

Then, after getting a good feel for this beautiful place, head off to one or more of the sights in town, such as:

- Chapel Bridge – Lucerne's most iconic destination. There is no fee to cross this historic bridge. For some fun, stop in at the small gift shop midway across.

- Old Town – Most of Old Town is on the right bank of the Reuss River (the area south and across the river from the train station). The array of interesting streets and buildings here will provide numerous photo opportunities. This is also where some of the best dining opportunities may be found.

- Lion of Lucerne Monument: An inspiring carving of a lion built into a rock face and located just a short distance from Old Town.

- Spreur Bridge: This is another interesting, covered bridge over the Reuss River. Just a short distance west from the Chapel Bridge.

- Musegg Wall & Towers: Portions of the walls which had once protected the city. The walls are open to go to ramparts where great views of the city are available.

- Alpineum Museum: A large and impressive diorama which depicts scenes of the Swiss Alps.

- Glacier Garden: View remnants of former glacial activity during the previous ice age. Several interactive exhibits for children.

- Swiss Museum of Transport: This large museum is a bit out from the center of town, but is a fun spot to visit. You will need to either take a ferry, a cab, or the local train to visit it. The exhibits include actual aircraft, boats, cars, and trains. Adjacent to the museum is the Swiss Chocolate Adventure.

A Starting-Point Guide

Swiss Museum of Transport
A Great Family Adventure

How to Get to Lucerne from Zurich:

- Train: This is very easy to do. Numerous non-stop or direct trains leave the central Zurich train station daily and reservations are generally not required. The train takes 50 minutes and, when you arrive in Lucerne, you will find this to be an exceptionally convenient station to central Lucerne. For some added convenience, there is a shopping mall in the lower level not unlike the mall in the lower level of Zurich's train station.

- Tours: Generally are not needed if your sole goal is visiting Lucerne, but many tours are available out of Zurich. An advantage of taking a group tour is that some combine a visit to one of the local mountains (Pilatus, Rigi, or Titlis), which can greatly reduce travel planning and hassle.

- Cars: Again, not needed, but if you want to rent a car, the drive will take about 35 to 40 minutes. One huge plus to having a car is that you can easily add in a trip to Mt. Rigi or any one of several attractive towns en route. One negative is that parking in central Lucerne can be a challenge.

~ ~ ~ ~ ~ ~

Mt. Pilatus: This 6,983-foot mountain (2,128 meters) is very close to central Lucerne and it is easy to combine a visit to both in one day. While there are taller mountains nearby such as Mt. Titlis, this doesn't take away from the experiences and views enjoyed by a visit here.

The Mt. Pilatus visitor center, hotel, and cogwheel train terminal.
Photo Source: Zeledi - Wikimedia Commons

Once you are at the top, where there is also a hotel and restaurant, you will find a large visitor center, eating opportunities, and trails leading out from the main platform.

Traveling up and down the mountain is a big part of the fun. While you have several options for your mode of travel, including the option of taking a ferry to the cogwheel train base, the most popular is to take a cogwheel train one way, and a gondola the other. There are two primary route packages, the Silver Round Trip and the Gold Round Trip.

- **Golden Round Trip:** includes a ferry, cog railway, gondola, and bus to make all elements of the trip. (See map on next page.)

- **Silver Round Trip:** Essentially the same, but without the ferry ride. This option includes a train from Lucerne to/from Alpnachstad instead of a ferry. All other elements of the trip remain the same. This option is less expensive and generally faster and more available than taking the ferry.

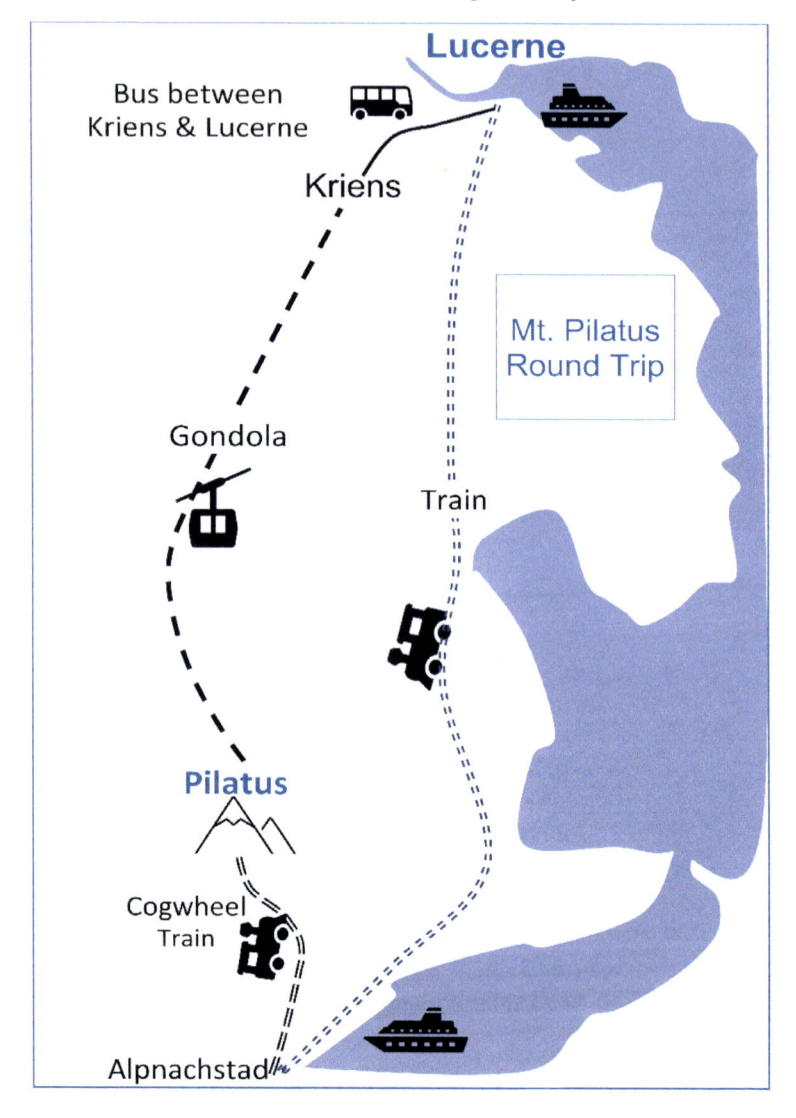

Lucerne

Bus between Kriens & Lucerne

Kriens

Mt. Pilatus Round Trip

Gondola

Train

Pilatus

Cogwheel Train

Alpnachstad

Mt. Pilatus viewed from Lucerne
Photo Source: Liridon - Wikimedia Commons

How to Get to Mt. Pilatus from Zurich: In addition to the trip to Lucerne, reaching the base of Mt. Pilatus will require an additional, but short, trip by train, bus, or ferry.

- Train: This is fairly easy to do. Trains to the base of the Mt. Pilatus Cogwheel train require two legs. The first is the train from Zurich to Lucerne, and the second is a short train trip from the Lucerne train station to Alpnachstad. This short train departs almost every hour. (Alternatives are to take the ferry from Lucerne to Alpnachstad or the bus to the gondola station in Kriens.)

- Tours: While not needed, some convenience can be realized by joining a tour group. Most of these tours will take you by bus or minivan directly from Zurich to the Pilatus cogwheel train station. When your mountain adventure is over, many tours also include a stop in Lucerne. The biggest downside for some is the loss of you being able to determine how much time you want to spend up on the mountain or in town. Still, there is a lot to be said for the added convenience and probably reduced travel time.

Mt. Rigi: Often referred to as "The Queen of the Mountains," this is the closest mountain to Zurich of the three outlined in this chapter (Rigi, Pilatus, Titlis). Mt. Rigi stands 5,897 feet (1,798 meters). At the top, you have excellent views of Lucerne and Lake Lucerne below you. There are also numerous hiking trails and a few areas to get a snack and small meal.

At the peak, in addition to the views and trails, there are also some pleasant surprises such as finding cows grazing near you with their melodic bells and quintessentially Swiss chalets dotting the hillsides.

Mt. Rigi - Viewed from Lucerne

How to Get to Mt. Rigi from Zurich: An easy and fun way to travel here is by train but note that this isn't the quickest as the total one-way trip can be around 90 minutes. If you drive directly to the base at Arth-Goldau, you will naturally save time. Tours are not necessary unless you want to include a trip to Lucerne with your trip to Mt. Rigi.

To take the train, there are two steps. The first is a train from Zurich's main station to Arth-Goldau. This train runs frequently. The second step is to ride the cogwheel train from the Arth-Goldau station up to the top of Mt. Rigi.

Mt. Rigi Website: www.Rigi.ch

Mt. Titlis: The tallest and most dramatic mountain detailed here it is also the furthest from Zurich, but still reasonably easy to reach for a one-day adventure. The mountain is an impressive 10,623 feet high (3,238 meters) and, when you arrive at the summit, you are treated to incredible views in every direction. For individuals who are from climates where snow does not appear, it can be a delight to be able to go out and play in the white stuff at any time of the year.

Mt. Titlis - viewed from the village of Engelberg at the base of the mountain.

The only negative about visiting this mountain is the crowds. So, if you come in the summer months, just be aware in advance that the gondolas and facilities at the top can be FULL of people from around the globe.

Once you are at the top, which takes multiple gondola legs, you will find an impressive facility with places to eat and numerous viewing stations. When you head

Bring a Jacket!

At any time of the year, even if it is hot down in Lucerne, it can be cold up here.

outside there are numerous activities including an ice cave and an enjoyable suspension bridge.

Mt. Titlis Cliff Walk

How to Get to Mt. Titlis from Zurich: A train trip to here requires around two hours' travel time each way from Zurich to the base town of Engelberg, and you will travel through Lucerne to do so. Once you reach Engleberg, it is then another thirty minutes or so to reach the top. So, with all of the travel components, it is generally best if you do not try to add in much or any time in Lucerne for your one-day adventure from Zurich.

If you drive or take a tour directly to here, there will be travel time savings of roughly one hour vs trains. If you travel by train, you will need to change trains in Lucerne. This may sound like a hassle, but it really isn't as Lucernes train station is easy to navigate. Also of note, if you come by train, you need to either travel by bus to the gondola station or take a pleasant ten-minute walk each way.

Mt. Titlis Website: www.Titlis.ch

Rhine Falls: Europe's largest waterfall. If you have ever been to Niagara Falls which straddles the US and Canadian border, you will find an incredible similarity to visiting here. there is a mixture

Rhine Falls - With Tour Boats at the Base of the Falls.

Rhine Falls Viewing Platform
Photo Source: Manecke - Wikipedia

of beautiful falls, hotels overlooking them, and numerous tourist activities including boat rides to the base of the falls.

Rhine Falls (Rheinfall in German). These falls are the most powerful in Europe. They are 490 feet wide (150 meters) and 75 feet high (23 meters). As you might guess by the name, the falls span the upper Rhine River. At this stage in the river's travels, it is an outflow from Lake Constance, Germany which is just a 25-minute drive east from here.

A Starting-Point Guide

Adjacent to the falls, is the attractive community of Neuhausen. Using Niagara Falls comparison again, there are attractions on both sides of the falls, but a majority of them are on the northern side. The good news is you can easily visit both sides as there is a long bridge near the falls which spans the river. One interesting note regarding this bridge is it is shared with the local train services.

> **Consider a Triangle Trip**
>
> It is easy to add in a visit to St. Gallen when visiting the falls and can be done by train, driving, or group tour.

What to See: In addition to the obvious attraction of simply viewing these falls, there are other fun ways to add to the adventure:

- Boat Trips: You can catch a boat which will take you not only to the base of the falls, but also to climb up a rocky protrusion in the middle of the falls.

- Adventure Trail: There is a recently added adventure trail complete with tunnels which take you down almost to water level.

- Viewing Platform: The Schloss Laufen platform brings you up close to the falls.

- Rhyfall Express: An open-air ride which takes you not only through the falls area but also into the neighboring Schaffhausen and its Old Town

Getting to Here: Travel to the falls is surprisingly easy regardless of the mode of travel you choose, or simply do it with a tour group which may also take you to St. Gallen or Leichtenstein.

- Driving: Takes roughly 40 minutes and there are several parking areas near the falls on either side.

- Train: There are two train stations near the falls with the closest being "Schloss Laufen am Rheinfall." It is a short walk to the falls from this station. Train travel will take around 45 minutes to one hour each way and trains leave about once an hour from Zurich.

Website: www.Rheinfall.ch

St. Gallen:[25] This attractive city of roughly 100,000 is in the northeastern portion of Switzerland and very close to the expansive Lake Constance. Sitting between rows of tall hills, the setting is beautiful. It also is an area with an unlimited array of outdoor activities. If you are one of the lucky few who can spend more than a day here, consider heading out to the hills for some excellent hiking opportunities.

St. Gallen and its charming Old Town

The focal point of St. Gallen is its Old Town (Altstadt). In addition to the expected array of quaint buildings, restaurants, and shops, you will find a beautiful monastery, a cathedral, and some intriguing museums such as a textile museum. (Textiles have historically been an important part of this city's economy.) This is largely a car-free area and there are many lanes to explore.

---

[25] **St Gallen Name:** Many reference sites, such as train travel sites, use the German name of *Sankt Gallen*.

Outside of the Old Town, and in the area around the train station, the feel changes dramatically to that of a modern and bustling city.

If you drive here, or join one of the many tours, chances are that the tour will include a visit to the area known as Appenzell. Don't pass this up as the area is classic Switzerland and often referred to as "Heidi Land." A fun destination here is the noteworthy Ascher Cliff Restaurant which sits precariously along a cliff face.

The famous Äscher Cliff Restaurant in the Appenzell area just south of St. Gallen.

What to See in Central St. Gallen:

- Old Town: This is largely a car-free section of town. In addition to the appealing narrow lanes, there are several plazas to explore with the Marktplatz being one of the largest and busiest.
- Cathedral, Abbey, & Abbey Library: St. Gallen's Abbey of St. Gall is a UNESCO listed treasure. Primarily an abbey, one of the most impressive portions of this huge complex to visit is the ornate library.

Easy Day Trips from Zurich

- Lapidarium: Adjacent to the Abbey Library, and in the underground vaults, is an intriguing array of art set in this medieval facility.
- Textile Museum: St. Gallen has a long history with textiles and even today this is an important product here. This museum speaks to that history with over 30 thousand objects on display.
- St.Laurenzen Church Tower: This is an 800 year old church near the cathedral and abbey. Even though the church's origins are old, the church has been largely rebuilt. Visitors can climb up the tall tower for excellent views of the city and area.

Getting to Here: Travel to St. Gallen from Zurich is easy by car, train and tour.

- Driving: Takes roughly 1 hour. Be sure to include some time to explore Appenzel along your drive.
- Train: There are numerous trains daily and most are direct. Expect travel time a bit over an hour each way. Once you arrive in St. Gallen, it is about a 10-minute pleasant walk to the abbey and the heart of Old Town.

St. Gallen Website: Stadt.sg.ch

Footnote From the Author: I hope you have found this guide to be helpful in planning your visit. Comments and suggestions for improvement, or notes on any errors found, are always appreciated. Feel free to pass along any suggestions you may have to my email at cincy3@gmail.com

Appendix: Helpful Online References

To help you expand your knowledge of this area, several online reference sites are listed here. Zurich is a popular city to visit, so there is a wealth of materials which can help in planning your trip.

The following is a list of online references about this city and area. The purpose of this list is to enhance your understanding of this area before embarking on your trip. Any online search will result in the websites outlined here plus many others. These are listed as they are professionally done and do not only try to sell you tours.

I.	Zurich City and Area Websites & Apps
Website Name	**Website Address and Description**
Zurich City	www.Zuerich.com Zurich city and area website including the Tourist Office. Your best overall resource for services, tours, lodging, and attractions in Zurich
Zurich Apps	Numerous excellent apps are available for Zurich and this area including: • Zurich City Guide • Zurich Transit • Zurich Map & Walks
City & Swiss Discount Cards	Several discount cards are available including the Zurich Card and Swiss Travel • www.Zeurich.com for the Zurich Card • www.Swiss-Pass.ch for the Swiss Travel Pass

Helpful Online Resources

I.	Zurich City and Area Websites & Apps
Website Name	**Website Address and Description**
Zurich Football / Soccer	www.FCZ.ch Learn about Zurich's professional football/soccer stadium and game schedule.
Major Events	Zurich has multiple large events each year. These sites detail some of the more notable ones: • Film Festival – www.zff.com • Street Parade – www.StreetParade.com • Carnival – www.ZurichCarneval.ch
You Tube	Several helpful videos available. One of the best is under the search term "Places to see in Zurich"
Wikipedia	www.Wikipedia.org - OR simply do a search for Zurich Wikipedia and this site will appear on most search results pages. Detailed information on Zurich's history and the city's early development.

II.	Zurich Museums and Attractions
Museum / Attraction	**Website**
Boat Rentals	Several companies rent boats and other water equipment here. Two of the leading sites are: • www.Lago-Zuerich.ch • www.BootsVermietung-Seefeld.ch
Falsenegg Mountain	www.Falsenegg.com

II.	Zurich Museums and Attractions
Museum / Attraction	**Website**
Fraumunster Church	www.Fraumuenster.ch
FIFA Museum	www.FifaMuseum.com
Grossmunster Church	www.GrossMuenster.ch
Kunsthaus Art Museum	www.Kunsthaus.ch
Lindt Chocolates	www.Lindt-Home-of-Chocolate.com
Rietberg Art Museum	www.Rietberg.ch
St. Peter Church	www.St-Peter-zh.ch
Swiss National Museum	www.LandesMuseum.ch
Uetilberg Mountain	www.Zuerich.com
Zoo	www.Zoo.ch

III.	Area Towns and Day Trips
Area	**Website Address and Description**
Liechtenstein	Two websites provide details on this small country: • www.Liechtenstein.li • www.Tourismus.li

Helpful Online Resources

III.	Area Towns and Day Trips
Area	**Website Address and Description**
Lucerne	www.Luzerne.com
Mt. Rigi	www.Rigi.ch
Mt. Titlis	www.Titlis.ch
Rhine Falls	www.Rheinfall.ch
St. Gallen	Stadt.sg.ch

IV.	Transportation Information and Apps
Website Name	**Website Address & Description**
Airport Transportation	This is one of the more notable ground transportation services from the Zurich airport. • www.7x7.ch
Zurich Airport	Details on the airport, its layout, ground transportation, and flight schedules: • www.Flughafen-Zuerich.ch
Apps for Transportation	Some of the leading apps to help with your travel planning include: • Rome2Rio • Trip Advisor • Switzerland Mobility
Bicycle Rental	This firm is aligned with the Zurich transportation network and also rents bikes in other cities. www.PubliBike.ch

A Starting-Point Guide

IV.	Transportation Information and Apps
Website Name	Website Address & Description
Swiss & Zurich Train Systems	Different websites and their apps provide guidance on train travel in Zurich and throughout Switzerland: • SBB Trains - www.SBB.ch • Zurich transportation system: www.ZVV.com
Lake ZurichFerries	www.ZSG.ch This site covers local buses, trams, bike rentals, and the two funiculars.
Train Ticket Resellers	Several services enable you to purchase train tickets online prior to your trip, including: - SBB.CH - RailEurope.com - Rome2rio.com - TrainLine.com - Eurorailways.com
Water Taxis	www.WasserTaxi.ch

V.	Tour and Hotel Booking Sites
Service	Website address and Description
Hotel Sites	Numerous online sites enable you to review and book hotels online. Most of these sites also resell tours. - Booking.com - Hotels.com - Expedia.com - Travelocity.com

Helpful Online Resources

Service	Website address and Description
V.	**Tour and Hotel Booking Sites**
Tour Companies & Resellers	Many companies, such as the ones listed here, provide a full variety of tours to Zurich as well as day tours. - Zuerich.com - SwissDayTours.com - Switzerland-Tour.com - WowZurich.com - GetYourGuide.com - ToursByLocals.com - Viator.com
Trip Advisor	*www.TripAdvisor.com* One of the most comprehensive sites on hotels and tours. Direct connection with Viator, a tour reseller.

Index

Airport Info............................37
Apps to Download 12
Area Covered 7
Art Museum....................79, 85
Ascher Cliff Restaurant 120
Attractions in Zurich..............67
Bahnhofstrasse 75
Bicycle Rentals.....................55
Boat Rentals.........................88
Central Zurich.......................23
Chagall Windows..................77
Chapel Bridge Lucerne.......109
Chinese Garden 89
Chocolate Factory 93
Christmas Market 32
Climate Overview 28
Clocktower 76
Currency...............................14
Day Tour Operators............101
Day Trip Ideas......................99
Districts in Zurich..................19
Dolder Grand Resort 59
Elevation for Zurich 17
Escherhöle Park...................83
Felsenegg Mountain.............92
Ferry Travel....................55, 95
Festivals and Events 30
FIFA Museum.......................84
Film Festival 32
Fraumunster.........................77
Funicular-Polybahn 71
Grossmünster Church 78
Hotels in Zurich 57
Itinerary Suggestions............ 8
Kunsthaus Museum..............79
Lake Cruises 97
Lake Zurich Details...............94
Landesmuseum....................70
Liechtenstein 103
Limmatquai...........................73
Lindenhof 24
Lindenhof Overlook 74, 75
Lindt Chocolate Museum......93
Lodging Suggestions............57
Lucerne Day Trip................106
Mountain Adventures 90, 92, 111, 114, 115
Mt. Pilatus Visit...................111
Mt. Rigi Daytrip...................114
Mt. Titlis Daytrip 115
Museum Rietberg.................85
Niederdorf Old Town 71
Old Town Zurich 69
One Day in Zurich 9
Points of Interest List............67
Polybahn Funicular...............71
Protestant Church 76
PubliBike 55
Quainanlagen Waterfront 86

Index

Rhine Falls 117
Rietberg Museum 85
Roman Baths 25
Seebad Water Park 88
Shopping Street 75
Soccer Museum 84
Soccer Team 27
Spring Festival 31
St. Gallen 119
St. Peter Church 76
Street Parade....................... 32
Striezelmarkt........................ 32
Swiss National Museum....... 70
Swiss Travel Pass 44
Tour Companies 46
Tourist Office 12
Tours of Zurich..................... 47
Train Station 34

Trams in Zurich 51
Transportation Tickets 54
Travel Apps.......................... 14
Travel Guidance 33
Travel in Zurich 49
Travel Passes 40
Uetilberg Mountain............... 90
Vaduz, Liechtenstein.......... 103
Walking Times 50
Water Fountains 26
Water Taxis.......................... 97
Waterfalls........................... 117
Waterfront Attractions 86
Women's Church 77
Zoo....................................... 83
Züri Velo Bike Rental 56
Zurich Card 41
Zurichhorn Park 89

Starting-Point Travel Guides

www.StartingPointGuides.com

This guidebook on Zurich is one of several current and planned *Starting-Point Guides*. Each book in the series is developed with the concept of using one enjoyable city as your basecamp and then exploring from there.

Current guidebooks are for:

Austria:
- Salzburg, and the Salzburg area.

France:
- Bordeaux, Plus the surrounding Gironde River region
- Dijon Plus the Burgundy Region
- Lille and the Nord-Pas-de-Calais Area.
- Lyon, Plus the Saône and Rhône Confluence Region
- Nantes and the western Loire Valley.
- Paris Day Trips by train from Paris.
- Reims and Épernay the heart of the Champagne Region.
- Strasbourg, and the central Alsace region.
- Toulouse, and the Haute-Garonne area.

Germany:
- Cologne & Bonn
- Dresden and the Saxony State
- Stuttgart and the and the Baden-Württemberg area.

Spain:
- Camino Easy: A mature walker's guide to the popular Camino de Santiago trail.

- Toledo: The City of Three Cultures

Sweden:
- Gothenburg Plus the Västra Götaland region.

Switzerland:
- Basel & Bern and nearby city and mountain adventures.
- Geneva, Including the Lake Geneva area.
- Lucerne, Including the Lake Lucerne area.
- Zurich – And the Lake Zurich area.

Fiction

Blue Water Bedlam
Murphy's Law has nothing on these guys!

Charlie just wanted to have some fun with his new boat and share that fun

Four retired guys set forth on a boating adventure north from the beautiful Puget Sound. Knowing nothing about what it takes to handle a yacht and the news of a recent murder on board doesn't stop them.

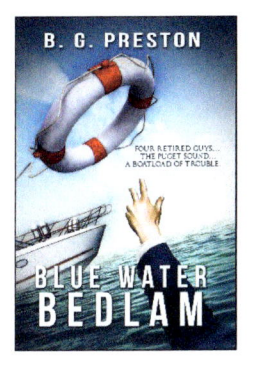

Camino Passages
Outdoor Adventure – Travel – Spain – Romance

The Camino de Santiago is an historical trail across northern Spain which provides hikers with an incredible variety of architectural, natural, and cultural delights. It also is, as Larry Adams learns, a wonderful social journey as well.

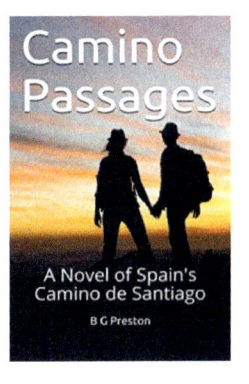

Setting out for Spain, Larry is only seeking a solo adventure and a much-needed change of pace. What Larry encounters during his walk are experiences and new relationships that could change his life forever.

Obsidian Portal
A story of adventure and discovery.
Four friends simply planned to kick back and relax, until half of a fish was found on the carpet.

Their simple discovery leads the group on an exciting quest. Have they uncovered a way to instantly transport people? They may have stumbled upon a whole new technology with astounding implications. Could it change the course of world economics and stir up a lot of trouble in the process?

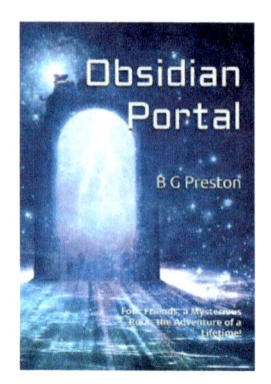

Portal Lost
Adventure & survival in an untamed world.

A morning commute turns out to be far from normal when Amy Scott steps out from a portal to find herself in a strange world!

Portal Lost tells the exciting story of a band of hardy individuals who quickly change from living in a modern society to living in a rugged wilderness...or die trying.

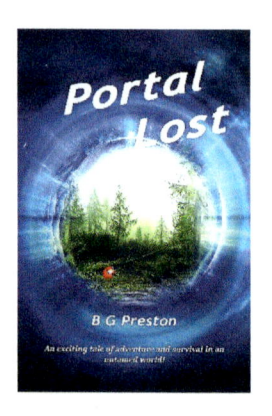

~ ~ ~ ~ ~

Updates on these and other titles may be found on the author's Facebook page at: www.Facebook.com/BGPreston.author

Feel free to use this Facebook page to provide feedback and suggestions to the author or email to: cincy3@gmail.com

Printed in Great Britain
by Amazon